Power in America

Power in America

The Southern Question and the Control of Labor

John F. Keller

VANGUARD
BOOKS

© 1983 by John F. Keller
All rights reserved

ISBN 0-917702-14-X

Photo Credits
Front cover photo by United Press International
Back cover photo by Khan

Library of Congress Catalog Card Number:
83-50412

Published by Vanguard Books
P.O. Box 3566, Chicago, Il. 60654

Printed in the United States of America

To my grandmother

Contents

List of Illustrations	ix
Preface	xi
Acknowledgements	xv

1. The National Question in History   1
   The Materialist Conception of History   2
   Capitalism and the Rise of Nations   2
   England's Multi-National Political Model   6
   The Multi-National System in the United States   11

2. National Development of the North and South   15
   National Development in the Western Hemisphere   16
   Confederation of the North American Colonies   21
   Conflict Over the Land Question   23
   National Development of the South   25
   Southern Nationalism and Northern Secessionism   31
   National Development of the North   35
   Northern Nationalism and Southern Secessionism   37
   The Colonization of the South   41

CONTENTS

3. The South as an Economic Reserve — 51
   The Theory of Political-Economic Realignment — 54
   Economic Realignments in U.S. History — 57
   Political Realignments in U.S. History — 63
   Crises, Wars, and the Realignment Cycle — 72
   The South in the Multi-National Economy — 83

4. The South as a Political Reserve — 99
   Capital, Labor, and Revolutionary Crises — 100
   Labor Revolts and Third Parties — 107
   The Theory of the Southern Strategy — 112
   The Two-Party System Through the Civil War — 118
   The Two-Party System Since Reconstruction — 124

5. The Color Question in the South — 135
   Basis of the Solid South — 137
   Factors in Southern Nationalism — 140
   Controlling the Southern Labor Movement — 142
   New Conditions in the South — 154
   The International Significance of the South — 158
   New Implications for Northern Labor — 163

Appendices — 169

References — 177

Bibliography — 185

Name Index — 191

Subject Index — 193

Illustrations

Figures

1. Importance of Cotton to the U.S. Economy, 1810-1930   26
2. North-South Income Differential, 1974   49
3. Major Forms of Capital in Different Party System Periods   58
4. The Rise and Decline of Industry Groups   60
5. Party Systems and Critical Crises   64

Maps

Core and Peripheral Areas of the Modern South
(with aerospace/electronics centers)   98

Appendices

A. Business Recessions and Depressions in
the United States, 1796—Present   169
B. Capital Trends Data Sheet   170
C. Major Wars in U.S. History, 1776—1973   171
D. Textile Spindles in the South, 1880—1976   172
E. Average Annual Textile Wages, 1921—1929   172
F. Lumber Production by Regions, 1869—1919   173
G. Apparel Industry Employment by Region, 1950—1974   173
H. Leading Industries by Value Added (1975)   174
I. Prime Military Contracts by Region, 1939-1981   175
J. Third Party Seats in Congress, 1789—1976   176

Preface

In the United States today we are experiencing an economic crisis of proportions without parallel since the 1930s. Along with this has developed the unprecedented danger of a world nuclear war. These conditions are causing working men and women to question the viability of our economic system, a system whose periodic collapse exacts an unbelievable toll in human suffering and which now threatens the future of all humanity.

Many of these questions touch on contemporary economic, political, and military issues and are questions of historic importance. Does every generation have to suffer through these crises? Will it take another war to revive the economy? Would we survive? Why have our political representatives been incapable of putting an end to these crises? Is a change in our basic system what is really needed? If so, why have we never been successful in changing this system in the past? What must the average person start doing to make sure this situation never develops again? If you are one of these questioning people, then this book is for you.

I have written this book out of concern for our future. As a social scientist, I have spent years studying the United States because I am convinced that the fate of billions of people depends on the decisions that one hundred million adult Americans in the most powerful country on earth make about our own future.

It is clear that more and more people are ready for a fundamental change in the way our country is economically and politically organized. But to change society, one must first understand how it is structured and why it periodically breaks down. In this book I do not attempt to say how to change society; rather I try to show what the main roadblocks are to revolutionizing the social system of the United States. With this kind of understanding, people can then develop their own strategies for change.

This is a book about how the economic and political system in this country has developed over the years and why we have repeatedly experienced devastating crises like the one today. It explains why working men and women in this country have never developed the political clout necessary to establish a full-employment economy at peace with the world. Such a discussion must be framed in terms of the economic classes in society and how their different interests diverge in times of crisis. In a sense it was inevitable that in the current crisis President Reagan would himself bring back into common usage the term "capitalist," which during the preceding boom times had been largely eliminated from government and press usage so as not to alienate "workers."

Now the crisis itself is alienating labor and the representatives of capital have been forced to appeal as one class to another for labor's help in saving the system. The old saying that "What is good for General Motors is good for the country" has been reincarnated as "What is good for Chrysler's investors is good for its workers." But who owes what to whom?

Because this book is framed by the concepts of capital, labor, and exploitation, some people will complain that this discussion is partisan and slanted. In fact, the discussion of crises, their origins, and what to do about them has always been restricted to elite circles of leaders in this country, and every past effort to reform the system and prolong its life has reflected their pro-capitalist bias. In the interests of true democracy, I have addressed this book specifically to all working men and women of the United States and have focused on your interests in these matters.

During serious economic crises in U. S. history, the conditions have been ripe for working people to take political matters in hand and reshape the economy on a non-competitive, non-private property basis free from the inevitability of mass unemployment and war. In every instance, however, powerful financial interests have thwarted the independent political development of the labor move-

PREFACE

ment, maintained political power for themselves, and perpetuated a competitive, crisis-oriented economy geared for private gain at public expense.

There is an explanation for how the representatives of capital have been successful at holding political power. The secret lies in a simple political formula which has been developed, mastered, and used to the advantage of capital. As the economy has changed over the past two hundred years, new financial interests have replaced old, but none has ever dominated the much larger, non-propertied working population without mastering this fundamental formula for political power. The key to this formula is the economic and political control of the South. Thus, labor is confronted with the problem I call the Southern Question.

This book explains how this formula is used to maintain political power for capital. No specific tactical recommendations will be found here, although the overall strategy for working class political power is necessarily suggested by the results of the analysis. The central problem for working men and women today is how to independently gain and exercise political power in this country. But only by first understanding the secret behind the political power of capital and the historical impotence of labor can an appropriate course of action be determined.

The issue of political power and the implementation of new economic and social policies are immediate concerns in the United States because of the devastation being wrought by the economic depression. But given the militarization of our economy and the dangerous talk of "winning" a nuclear war, all of the world's peoples are anxiously watching our course of action.

History has now pushed the worker in the United States to center stage in the dramatic quest for world peace, prosperity, and equality. This book is a personal contribution to clarifying the political problems we face in that quest and to pointing the way out.

J. F. K.
South Hadley, Mass.
May 1983

Acknowledgements

There are literally thousands of individuals who have struggled for an understanding of the Southern Question and its meaning for the working class movement in the United States. It would be impossible to acknowledge all of them.

Among those key individuals who—as links in this chain—were most responsible for enlightening me about this issue and its centrality to the political future of labor in the United States are W. E. B. Du Bois, Harry Haywood, and Nelson Peery, all of whose work I have had occasion to quote herein. I have tried to continue their work and further their analyses, and I acknowledge the seminal role played by their ideas.

I also want to take this opportunity to acknowledge the fine work of all the members of the Vanguard Books editorial and production departments, whose sustained effort under a great deal of pressure made this book a reality. Our mutual effort attests to our belief in the importance of this book.

Power in America

1.

The National Question in History

The object of this book is to explain the general **political formula** by which a succession of powerful financial interests have maintained control of the federal government throughout U.S. history. This control by a relatively small but elite social class has allowed the perpetuation of an economic system designed to serve private rather than public interests. Labor has no effective say in establishing economic or even labor policy. Should labor resist the decisions of this financial elite, the latter has the power of the **state**—the police, courts, prisons, and even the army—to enforce its decisions.

In his famous works on military science Clausewitz wrote that war is an extension of politics. It is equally true that politics is an extension of economics. **Political economy** provides the framework for analyzing human history. It is the core of the **materialist theory of history**, which says that all political change occurs as a result of changes in the economic system and that once a political system has developed, it serves to maintain the status quo in economic relations. If the economic system is based on private property and the private control of banks and industry, then the government will always act to protect these private interests.

Only by first understanding how a particular economic class maintains political power and uses that power to reinforce its economic interests can the labor movement begin to chart its own strategy for defeating that political force, exercising its own political power, and reorganizing society in the economic interest of the vast majority of working men and women.

The Materialist Conception of History

There are two aspects to the materialist conception of history. The **structural aspect** indicates that political systems serve to defend and maintain the economic status quo and the advantages of one economic class over another. In societies in which the economic system is organized on a non-class basis (for example, in most hunting/gathering and tribal societies and in modern countries organized along socialist lines), the political system is meant to support collective sharing in the fruits of the economy by all and to restrict private gain by a few at the expense of others.

The **evolutionary aspect** indicates that the spontaneous invention of new tools, technologies, and production methods results in the development of new economic systems characterized by new economic classes who either operate or own these productive forces. No matter how stubbornly a political system tries to prolong the existence of an old economic system, at some point people realize they have to break with the old political system and replace it with a new one designed to promote and maintain a new system of economic relations based on the advances in production. These periods of upheaval are called **revolutions** and are normal events in the process of human social evolution.

The rise of a new economic system and a new political system yields what is called a **political-economic formation**. In the course of human history there have been only a handful of different political-economic formations.

Capitalism and the Rise of Nations

The United States is a society with an economic system based on private ownership of banks and industries. The masses of working people have no share in the ownership and control of these economic institutions. Since the late 1800s capitalist enterprises have become highly concentrated and monopolized. Today the decisions of a board of directors acting in the interest of private financial backers can throw tens or hundreds of thousands of workers into the streets.

This reveals a serious contradiction between the highly **collectivized production** of modern industrial economies and the lingering **private ownership** of the economy. Production decisions are invariably based on the prospects for turning a profit, with little or no consideration given to the masses of people suddenly turned out of their jobs. This naturally raises two questions: how to better organize the economy and how to politically implement these changes in organization. The highly collectivized and socialized nature of the production process suggests the direction these changes must take.

The object here is to describe how the current political system functions to prevent the reorganization of U.S. society. The problem is to show how the **structural** nature of this political-economic system has blocked and continues to block the **revolutionary** transformation of U.S. society. To understand the origins and class character of U.S. society, the rise of our country must be placed in historical perspective.

Since the beginning of human history the focus of political-economic development has shifted from place to place around the globe. Several million years ago the human species began to evolve biologically in the vicinity of the modern country of Ethiopia. At least two hundred thousand years ago the control of fire, the manufacture of flaked stone tools, and the development of language and ritual signaled the rise of the first type of political-economic formation—hunting/gathering **bands**. From the circum-Mediterranean area human populations organized on the band model spread throughout Africa, through the Mideast into Europe and Asia, through Asia into the Pacific Islands, and across the Bering Strait into North and South America.

In the Old and New Worlds the domestication of plants and

4 THE NATIONAL QUESTION IN HISTORY

animals occurred independently in different places. But the leading edge of this agricultural revolution was in the Mideast. About twelve thousand years ago, hill-dwelling **tribes** developed rudimentary forms of political organization to collectively allocate and maintain land, water, and animal resources and to defend these fixed assets.

The invention of the wooden plow resulted in the introduction of draft animals into agriculture, and the possibility arose of bringing vast river valley bottomlands under cultivation. Such an unprecedented extension of production raised the prospect of surplus production, widespread trade, and the accumulation of wealth. It also required a much larger labor force. Previously, prisoners of tribal warfare had been executed because they were a drain on community resources. Now they were sold into slavery, and class divisions between propertied and property-less individuals appeared for the first time in human history.

On this economic class basis the first **city-state** political-economic formations appeared around seven thousand years ago in the vicinity of modern Iraq. Other "cradles of civilization" emerged in places ranging from the African Sudan to Peru. Wherever they arose, city-state governments organized the conquest of peripheral tribal peoples and established colonial systems from which they extracted tribute. The most important city-state system in European history was the Roman Empire.

With the invention of the iron plow, centuries of expansion and conquest ended in the decentralization of the Roman city-state economy. This system was replaced by numerous **feudal domains** ruled by a landlord class. In these political-economic formations formerly enslaved tribal villagers were transformed into semi-free peasant farmers. They were allowed enough independence to enable this decentralized system to work. This process began in Europe about fourteen hundred years ago and was repeated throughout India, China, and Japan.

As a result of the greater play given to personal initiative among working people in feudal society, an array of new handicraft techniques developed and flourished. The congregation of handicraft specialists in feudal towns and trading centers set the stage for the rise of a historically new type of political-economic formation. In European towns in the 1600s individual craft techniques evolved into more complex manufacturing processes. Most required skilled labor organized in the form of guilds. Later the invention of the steam engine and the power loom made possible a mass-production industrial system based on unskilled labor. Peasants who fled the grip of feudal landlords or who were forced off land fenced in for pasture flooded into towns to take work as "free" **wage laborers**. But like their peasant and slave ancestors they remained subordinate to another class of people who owned and controlled the means of production—the original town dwellers. The latter came to be called "burghers" in Germany, the "bourgeoisie" in France, and just plain "businessmen" in England. This economic class controlled **capital** and industry then, and their descendants still do today.

European industrial cities arose in the late 1700s and early 1800s and produced clothing and agricultural equipment for the mass of people still living in the countryside. In turn, the countryside fed the cities and funneled labor into them. This division of labor between town and country became a hallmark of what are called **national markets**. Each developed its own national language of economic exchange as well as a national culture reflecting social life within that market. Competition for political control of national territories typically culminated in national revolutions by the urban economic classes. These were led by businessmen who allied with the peasantry against the political power of the old feudal aristocracy. When victorious, the arising business interests consolidated their political power over a national territory through the creation of a nation-state. In 1609 the Republic of Holland became the first example of this new type of political-economic formation, the **nation**.

The world process of national development continued with the English and French revolutions. Their colonization of the New World led to a shift in the focus of national development to North America in the late 1700s, as evidenced by the War of Independence. In the early 1800s the revolt of Spain's colonies in the New

World resulted in the formation of more than twenty Latin American nations. In the late 1800s the center of national development shifted to central and southeast Europe and to Asia. With World War I came the collapse of the main feudal states in these areas. Since World War II the process of national development has centered in Africa and the Middle East. Now all the world's peoples are organized in nations and this stage of human social development has run its course.

The first attempts at organizing society in a new way have already begun, as evidenced by the **socialization** of banks and industries in countries on every continent. However, the United States has maintained the particular class structure characteristic of nations. It is also the most powerful country on earth and has the unparalleled economic and military means to retard the transition of human society to its next phase.

Crises like the one being experienced in the 1980s indicate that the United States itself is ready for a change. To effect this change one needs to understand how business interests in the country maintain their political dominance and block social progress. Like many things in U.S. culture, the model for political power here is derived from English history.

England's Multi-National Political Model

Although the 1609 national revolution in Holland preceded that in England by about forty years, England soon became the more powerful of the two nations. One of the early characteristics of English national development was the simultaneous effort to control the economies of the other nations developing alongside England on the British Isles.

The Welsh people had been conquered by feudal England and were automatically retained within her capitalist political system after the English national revolution of 1649.

To the north and west the nations of Scotland and Ireland were also developing. By the Acts of Union of 1707 and 1800 both

Scotland and Ireland were forcibly subordinated to the English nation. Their national markets were turned into colonies under the control of English business interests, and their governments were incorporated into the English parliamentary system. This type of political-economic system is called a **multi-national state**.

This "United Kingdom" was held intact by military force. To this day England has been entangled in numerous wars to put down independence movements on the British Isles, especially in Ireland and now in northern Ireland. Indeed the **Irish question** was (and still is) key to the strength of the capitalist class in England and its ability to maintain political power over the English working class.

How could the colonial status of Ireland work against the interests of English workers? This was precisely the question which the General Council of the International Workingmen's Association (IWA) asked itself in 1869. The IWA was the first international organization of trade union leaders in world history. It existed during the world crisis which began with the Civil War in the United States, culminated in the revolt of the French working class in 1871 (the Paris Commune), and ended with the defeat of the Reconstruction governments in the U.S. South in 1876.

The IWA was governed by representatives from the labor movements in Europe and North America, but it was based in Europe and the majority of its members were Europeans. The IWA sought to unite the labor movements in the different capitalist countries so that workers in one nation would not be pitted against workers of other nations either in economic competition or in war.

At that time the English working class was the largest and most powerful in Europe, and the IWA could accomplish little without the agreement and leadership of the English labor movement. But while the English working class had the potential to lead an international movement for peace and socialism (which was then a new issue on the continent) it was also an accomplice in the national oppression of another working class, the Irish working class. Thus whenever the IWA pushed for unity of action of the international labor movement, the English working class resisted because of its position on the Irish question. The English workers sided with capital against one section of the international labor movement and therefore undermined the efforts of the IWA.

This impediment to the goals and objectives of the IWA forced the organization to deal with the theoretical problem of how the capitalist class in England was able to keep the allegiance of the English working class on this question. Only by understanding the problem **theoretically** could the IWA hope to show the English workers the **practical** implications of siding with the capitalists on this issue of world importance.

After prolonged study the IWA made a tremendous breakthrough in the analysis of the Irish question. It analyzed the method of political rule in England and the implications for the English working class. That analysis was recorded in the minutes of the General Council of the IWA in 1870.

> England alone can serve as the **lever** for a serious **economic** revolution. It is the only country where there are no more peasants and where land property is concentrated in a few hands. It is the only country where the **capitalist form**, i.e., combined labor on a large scale under capitalist masters, embraces virtually the whole of production. It is the only country **where the great majority of the population consists of wage laborers**. It is the only country where the class struggle and organization of the working class by the **Trades Unions** have **acquired** a certain degree of maturity and universality. It is the only country where, because of its domination on the world market, every revolution in economic matters must immediately affect the whole world. If landlordism and capitalism are classical examples in England, on the other hand the **material conditions** for their **destruction** are the most mature there.
>
> England cannot be treated simply as a country along with other countries. She must be treated as the **metropolis of capital**.[1]

Having realized the leading role of the English labor movement in guiding the political activity of workers in other industrial countries, the General Council passed to the question of how English capital maintained its political hegemony over the working class on the basis of the Irish question. Ireland was a source of cheap wool and meat for clothing and feeding English workers. It was also a source of immense profits for business. Political representatives of the capitalists captured the political leadership of the working class by arguing that it was in the interests of the workers to help maintain control over this cheap source of daily needs. But by adopting this position English workers weakened their own political voice.

If England is the bulwark of landlordism and European capitalism, the only point where one can hit official England really hard **is Ireland**.
In the first place Ireland is the **bulwark** of English landlordism.... Landlordism in Ireland is maintained solely by the **English army**. The moment the **forced union** between the two countries ends... English landlordism would not only lose a great source of wealth, but also its **greatest moral force**, i.e., that of representing the domination of England over Ireland. On the other hand, by maintaining the power of their landlords in Ireland, the English proletariat makes them invulnerable in England itself.[2]

Thus Ireland was a controlled **political reserve** which gave the English landlords and capitalists steady representation in Parliament and control of key committees and policy making. The domination of Ireland also provided capital with the **ideological weapon** to undermine any unity of action which might have developed among English and Irish workers in common opposition to English capital.

[T]he English bourgeoisie has not only exploited the Irish poverty to keep down the working class in England by **forced immigration** of poor Irishmen, but it has also divided the proletariat into two hostile camps.... The average English worker hates the Irish worker as a competitor who lowers wages and the **standard of life.** He feels national and religious antipathies for him. He regards him somewhat like the **poor whites** of the Southern States of North America regard their black slaves. This antagonism among the proletarians of England is artifically nourished and supported by the bourgeoisie. It knows that **this scission is the true secret of maintaining its power.**[3] [last emphasis added]

While national hostilities were kept alive by newspaper editors and church leaders who continually harped on the supposed "threat" posed to the English worker by the Irish worker, the government's solutions for controlling Ireland posed their own threats to the English working class.

Furthermore, Ireland is the only pretext the English Government has for retaining a **big standing army,** which, if need be, as has happened before, can be used against the English workers after having done its military training in Ireland.[4]

The fatal mistake of the English working class which prevented it from becoming an independent political force in English society was its decision to side with English business interests in colonizing other people. The analysis by the IWA concluded:

Any nation which oppresses another forges its own chains.
... [I]t is a **precondition to the emancipation of the English working class** to transform the present **forced union** (i.e., the enslavement of Ireland) into **equal and free confederation** if possible, into **complete separation** if need be.[5]

Not surprisingly, the two main North American countries derived from England—the United States and Canada—developed multi-national political structures patterned along the lines of the United Kingdom. And the working classes in the Northern and

Southern United States and in English and French-speaking Canada have been kept similarly divided and powerless.

The Multi-National System in the United States

For more than two centuries after her national revolution England dominated world industrial production and trade. Her armies and colonists settled vast lands in North America, conquered the southern and eastern coasts of Africa, and controlled colonies as far away as India and Australia. But England's dominance could not survive the intense international competition which developed in the second half of the 1800s. The Civil War in the United States and the 1870 Franco-Prussian War in Europe marked the emergence of three new competitors for England's world market. The United States proved to be the most formidable of these competitors.

> The "Americanization" of Europe and the far places of the earth advances.... We were Britain's colony once. She will be our colony before she is done, not in name, but in fact. Machines gave Britain power over the world. Now better machines are giving America power over the world....
> What chance has Britain against America? Or what chance has the world?[6]

England originally grew strong on the basis of the textile industry. But the Civil War and the Franco-Prussian War provided the conditions for the rapid development of many new technical and industrial means needed to win those wars. On this basis the industrial development of the United States, France, and Germany surged forward. Then in the massive world crisis of the 1890s England's trade links with her colonial markets began to weaken. This weakening continued right through World War I as England withdrew capital from abroad in order to prepare for and finance a war at home. Into this breach stepped the United States as the world's rising new power.

The Civil War not only brought about the emergence of the United States as an industrial power but also formalized the organization of this country as a multi-national state. The history of the United States prior to the Civil War was the history of the development of **two distinct nations**—one in the North and one in the South—confederated under one government. Each nation developed on a different economic basis with a different national market and culture. The Civil War marked the political separation of these nations into separate national states.

Nations are essentially a product of rising capitalism. Capitalist production is the production of commodities on the basis of wage labor. The central feature distinguishing one nation from another is the existence of historically distinct **labor markets**. Of course, the national existence of the pre-Civil War South was predicated on a system of cotton-producing slave labor which provided the foundation for other capitalist enterprise and commerce in the South as a whole. Slave labor had a definite restraining influence on the value of wage labor in the South and gave rise to the original differences between Northern and Southern labor markets.

The slave labor system also provided the basis for the overwhelming political power of the planters in the South. Together with their Northern Democratic counterparts, who represented cotton-financing and trading interests in the Northeast, Southern Democrats were able to shape economic policy in their interests.

They used the federal government to protect and enforce those interests to the detriment of rising industrial interests in the North. However, as the Northern economy developed and attracted immigrant labor, the balance of political power began to shift to the North. The Civil War marked the South's decision to separate itself politically from the federal system and to re-establish its dominance on the continent by issuing the North a military defeat.

Of course the North prevailed and forcibly retained the Southern nation within the federal system as "conquered provinces," to use the words of radical Republican Thaddeus Stevens. This was the origin of the **colonized** status of the South within the multi-national system of the United States. This relationship continues to this day, as evidenced by the differential operation of labor markets in the North and South (due especially to the Taft-Hartley Act and the system of Southern "right-to-work" laws). It is a multi-national system similar to the "United Kingdom" and the Canadian federation to which the French-speaking Quebec nation is subordinate.

Since the Civil War the most powerful industrial and financial interests in the United States have been based in the North. They pursue their interests through the political offices of either the Republican Party or the Northern wing of the Democratic Party. Their secret in attaining political power and maintaining it against the labor movement has been the mastering of this formula: **whoever controls the South can control the Northern labor movement and whoever controls labor can control the government.** Former President Calvin Coolidge put it most succinctly when he said: "Because the Democratic party has had the solid South without much regard to issues, it has [been able] to appeal to the [labor] radicals of the North. If it were to lose this strength it could not win."[7]

In other words, control of labor and government in the United States has hinged on control of the Southern wing of the Democratic Party. In practice this control is secured through the promise of **internal improvements** or other economic policies beneficial to the economy of the colonized South. Sometimes the Northern Democrats exercise control over this wing of their own party, but sometimes it is the Republicans who hold sway (just as the Reagan administration does today).

With Southern Democrats as a base, a political party can approach the powerful labor movement in the North and propose an electoral alliance which can win control of the government and supposedly push through legislation favorable to labor. However, once in power the political representatives of Northern capital can just as easily call on conservative, Southern-controlled congressional committees to block progressive economic legislation and push bills favorable to capital. Such a government also has never hesitated to use judicial and military force in repressing labor actions which arise in protest.

Because of this reliance on a Southern political base, Northern politicians in both major parties go to great lengths to maintain conservative Southern politicians in power. The key to accomplishing this has always been the **color question**. This political factor is used for crushing or coopting the progressive potential of the combined black and white vote in the Deep South in order to maintain conservatives in power.

Control of the black masses in the South is transformed into control not only of labor policy but also of foreign policy affecting billions of people—mostly people of color—throughout the world. The full formula for political power in the United States thus reads: **whoever controls the Southern black can control the South, whoever controls the South can control labor and the government, and whoever controls the U.S. government can control economic and political policy in the non-socialist world**. The fact that no decisions are taken at western summit conferences without U.S. consent bears this out.

On the basis of this general political formula the development of the independent **class interests** of workers in the United States has been thwarted and suppressed for over two hundred years. Since World War II and the rise of the United States to a dominant position in the political economy of the non-socialist world, it has also meant the repression of the labor movement in other countries by fascist governments openly supported by our political leaders.[8] The pre-Civil War lesson that "labor cannot emancipate itself in the white skin where in the black it is branded"[9] today holds true not only for the United States but also for much of the world.

Whether the domestic and international subordination of labor to capital persists much longer is in a very real sense up to the workers in the United States just as it was once up to the workers in England. The future for workers lies with that of other workers and not with capital. To understand how to break the political power of capital one must understand how it has been maintained so far. This system of political rule will be examined in detail in the following chapters.

2.

National Development of the North and South

Modern studies of the political economy and culture of the Deep South confirm the truly distinctive **national character** of this so-called region or section of the United States. Many of the best studies of the South describe its economy as a **colonized economy** within the boundaries of the United States. Rupert B. Vance's classic **Human Geography of the South** makes this point. So do the last two volumes of Louisiana State University's ten-volume history of the South (C. Vann Woodward's **Origins of the New South, 1877-1913** and George B. Tindall's **The Emergence of the New South, 1913-1945**), both of which have chapters on the South's colonized economy.

When one thinks of the Deep South in social scientific terms —that is, as a nation within the multi-national system of the United States—then the source of the persistently distinctive characteristics of the South becomes excitingly clear. Consider how the English literary critic Paul Binding described the moment of his realization that Southern literature is in fact a **national literature**.

"The South," wrote Reynolds Price in "Dodo, Phoenix, or Tough Old Cock," an essay on the Southern novel, "can come honorably out of a cool examination of its fiction in the past forty years. In fact its record as a country can stand with the simultaneous record of any country—with France, Britain, Germany, the rest of America.". . .

"As a country"—I remember the intellectual excitement I felt when I first read these significant words. They seemed to help answer a question that had been perplexing me for some time. The rollcall of Southern writers since 1920. . . is a most impressive one. . . . It hardly needs be said that. . . these masterworks could be (and indeed are) enjoyed and respected by readers with no knowledge of or concern for the South. This fact. . . at once removes the possibility of their being considered merely regional. For a regional writer is interesting **primarily** because of his relation to his particular area. Nevertheless, all these writers have set their work in the South, dealt with specific Southern issues or situations, and show themselves to be obsessed with Southern history and culture. . . .

But if one regards the writers as coming from a separate country—and after all, the South was once the independent Confederate States of America—then much of their curious position is explained. A serious novelist is usually concerned with the problems and culture of his own country, at the same time that he or she takes it for granted that the subject matter will be interesting and important to the readers. Thus the Southern writer can tackle plights peculiar to the South in terms that make them seem part of the world's experience.

Common nationality among writers means the sharing of important qualities."[1]

If the South is indeed a nation, then an examination of history should reveal details of separate national development in the North and South.

National Development in the Western Hemisphere

The rise of nations is coincident with the development of capitalist methods of production. **Nations** are simply the typical form of social community encompassing a capitalist class and a working class in a given territory. Between the time of the "discovery" of the Americas by Europeans in the 1490s and the rise of European competitors for England's world market in the late 1800s, the process of national development in the Western Hemisphere went through **three main stages**: colonization was followed by wars of independence and then by a period of inter-American warfare.

The first stage in this process involved roughly two hundred years of **colonization** by England (with the most economically advanced colonies), Spain (with the most extensive territorial holdings), Portugal, Russia, France, and Holland. Each of these powers penetrated the "New World" at distinct points, but altogether their actions constituted a mass colonization process over the length and breadth of the hemisphere. This stage was conditioned by intense conflict on the European continent between decaying feudalism and rising capitalism, with the new capitalists trying to consolidate strong national states, develop foreign resources and markets, and despoil each other of their new colonial domains.

In the course of colonization, European society transmitted to the colonies the capitalist way of organizing production and exchange and thus laid the basis for national development in the Western Hemisphere. By the late 1700s this process was far enough advanced that almost the whole of North and South America rose up in arms against colonial rule and for political independence. Thus began the second stage in the hemispheric process of national development, and by the mid-1800s a host of new independent nations had been established.

This stage—the establishment of states as a result of **national wars of independence**—unfolded in five main phases. First, the revolution in the more developed English colonies on the Atlantic seaboard culminated in their unification under a single federal state apparatus. Second, the Haitian Revolution of 1790-1803—the only successful slave insurrection in the history of the hemisphere —brought forth an independent republic. Third, the Brazilian Revolution of 1810-1822 ended in the unification of the fifteen

18 NATIONAL DEVELOPMENT OF THE NORTH AND SOUTH

states of Brazil as a republic called the United States of Brazil. Fourth, widespread revolt throughout the Spanish colonies, especially between 1810 and 1830, resulted in the dissolution of that huge colonial system and the formation of the independent states of Paraguay (1811), Argentina (1816), Chile (1818), Greater Colombia (including Venezuela and Ecuador, 1819), Peru (1821), the United Provinces of Central America (1823), the United States of Mexico (1824), Bolivia (1825), and Uruguay (1828). Fifth, the 1837 rebellions by Lower Canada (Quebec) and Upper Canada (Ontario) against England led to consolidation of the Quebec nation under the British colonial administration based in Ontario. Canada later gained independence as an English-style multi-national state with the Quebec nation held in a colonized status within Canada.

With the establishment of these independent national formations in the Western Hemisphere, a third stage of national development began. It was characterized by a round of **inter-American wars** which persisted roughly between 1825 and 1883. These wars were the direct result of efforts by the capitalist class in each new nation to solve its most pressing problem: how to secure and develop its home market. History shows that these economic struggles often escalated to the political and military sphere as competitors attempted to extend territorial boundaries or defend the sovereignty of their borders.

Some of the most important inter-American wars were the Brazil-Argentina-Uruguay War of 1825-1828, a second war fought over Uruguay between 1839 and 1851, the Mexico-United States War of 1846-1848, the Ecuador-Peru War of 1859, and the Pacific War of 1879-1883 between Chile, Peru, and Bolivia. In addition to these conflicts, the United States had territorial disputes with the last colonial powers on its borders. Between 1803 and 1867 the federal government—by military threat and negotiation —secured possession of the Louisiana Territory from France, Florida from Spain, northern Maine and the Oregon Territory from England, and Alaska from Russia.

The two greatest military struggles ever fought in the Western

Hemisphere occurred in the 1860s and marked the apex of the stage of inter-American wars. In South America there was the bloody Paraguay War of 1864-1870. In this war Paraguay was invaded by Brazil, Argentina, and Uruguay and lost five-sixths of its 1.3 million people. In North America the Civil War of 1861-1865 between the slave states and free states resulted in a half-million casualties.

What was the historical connection between these events? Andre Gunder Frank, a popular Latin American political-economist, has identified the common question. That question was whether the new nations of the Western Hemisphere would develop industrially self-sufficient **home markets** or remain raw material **export economies** dependent upon European manufactures. The civil wars of the mid-1800s resolved the question differently in North and South America.

> The immediate cause of [the North American] war between the manufacturing North and the cotton South was which of the two would prevail in their competitive expansion into the West. The victory of the North, albeit hard-won, must be attributed to the greater economic and particularly industrial power that it had already been able to develop. And this military victory opened the way to the continued, or renewed, westward expansion and development of industrial capitalism in the United States. The long-standing "tariff question" between the protectionist North and the free-trade South (and its British ally) was definitely answered in favor of nationalist industrial development protected by increasingly high tariffs. And "the South did not become less, but more heavily dependent on outside capital... it became even more a colony of the North than it had been before the Civil War." [Douglas Dowd in Harold D. Woodman, ed., **Slavery and the Southern Economy, Sources and Readings** (New York, 1966), 251.]

In Latin America the contemporary historical development was far different, although the productive forces and interests in conflict were not so different—but with their relative economic and political power in opposite proportions to those of North America. . . .

[In Latin America] the major agricultural and mining producers and exporters were economically and politically fortified by the trade liberalization before the turn of the nineteenth century and their appetite was whetted by this development while their annoyance grew with the remaining Spanish interference in and toll-taking from their business. These producers and merchants became the principal promoters and financers of the political movement for Independence from Spain in order to achieve state power and to be free to expand the raw materials export business—and thereby to increase Latin American economic dependence on the European, albeit now British, metropolis still more. . . .

[T]he Latin "Americans". . . from the provinces were those who sought to defend and develop the still remaining manufacturing industry and to promote Latin America's own development without the loans and other subordinating dependency relations with Europe, which the Europeans regarded as "enlightened" and which their Latin American economic partners and political allies among the raw materials export production interests perceived as the essence of "civilization." While Britain was systematically deindustrializing India, these rival economic and political forces still had several decades to fight this and other issues out in a series of bloody civil wars. In distinction to the United States, in Latin America these civil wars always ended with the final victory of the. . . raw materials producers and exporters.[2]

Frank goes on to detail why Paraguay was attacked so viciously. It was attempting (like the U.S. North) to independently develop a national industrial base and a railroad system to service the internal market. These developments were financed by national capital. The country was also being transformed socially by means of near-universal primary education. Just as the industrial North was perceived by the South as a threat to its existence, an industrialized Paraguay was regarded as a threat to its export-oriented neighbors. In both instances a pre-emptive blow was struck against the industrialists by the exporters. In North America this failed, but in South America the people of Paraguay—and their socio-economic experiment—were virtually exterminated.

Seen in the context of this process of national development, national revolution, and inter-national conflict which occurred throughout the hemisphere, the **Civil War in North America** appears neither as a "sectional" war (as many traditional historians describe it) nor as a capitalist revolution against Southern "feudalism" (as "old left" historians propose). This war marked the coming undone of the fragile political confederation of two distinct national formations which matured following the revolutionary war. This unstable confederation under one state had its origins in the politically expedient union of the thirteen colonies against England. The eventual military conflict between the North and South was the outcome of many years of unresolved political struggle for the sovereignty of their separate economic systems.

Confederation of the North American Colonies

The seaboard colonies of North America were the most economically advanced in the hemisphere—a reflection of the level of development of capitalism in England—and were the first to rebel against colonial rule. The first Continental Congress in 1774 discussed the coordination of resistance to English rule. The second Congress in 1775 declared a state of war and established an army. The colonies then declared their independence and constituted themselves as separate provinces. By mid-1776 rebellious **provincial congresses** backed up by armed Committees of Safety were strong enough to issue a joint Declaration of Independence.

In the ensuing revolutionary war, English military forces tried to reimpose control. In 1777 the Articles of Confederation were proposed by the provinces in an attempt to strengthen unity of action against England and to formalize the commitment of each province to provide a quota of troops for the army. However, the articles ensured that each province would remain politically sovereign. Action on the articles was tabled because the entry of France into the conflict on the side of the provinces tipped the military balance in their favor and forestalled the need for a more centralized form of organization.

Prior to the English surrender to provincial and French forces at Yorktown in 1781, it became questionable whether the politically fragmented provinces could conclude an internationally recognized treaty of peace and independence. English merchants seeking renewed trade with North America favored a peace treaty. However, political forces around the king were content to delay any settlement, regroup, and wait for a new chance at intervention (as occurred in 1812). The political and economic isolation of the provinces which was fostered during colonial rule was expected to work in England's favor. Therefore, some form of **confederation** seemed essential for the provinces to successfully confront England and conclude a peace.

The greatest political obstacle to confederation was the unresolved disposition of conflicting **land claims** by the provinces to unsettled western lands. Virginia claimed lands ranging from the Appalachians to the Mississippi and extending as far north as Lake Superior. Small provinces whose western borders had already been established feared the domination of the proposed confederation by those provinces with the largest land claims.

Maryland refused to ratify the Articles of Confederation until all land claims were placed in a **Public Domain**. This deadlock ended when New York ceded its claims and set a precedent for the other provinces. Virginia made clear its intention to follow suit, although with certain reservations later recognized by Congress in the Virginia Proviso of 1784.

Thus Maryland's objections were overcome, and the Articles of Confederation were finally ratified. On this basis the newly confederated but individually sovereign provinces were able to present a common political front to England. Two years of difficult negotiations finally culminated in the 1783 Treaty of Paris.

The nationalization of western lands also forged a temporary identity of contradictory interests among small farmer settlers, wealthy land speculators, and Southern planters, all of whom desired access to the new Public Domain. The land question has often been the basis for the convergence of **class interests** in U.S. history. In this instance this convergence of interests found political expression in the 1789 ratification of a constitution which provided for a strong central **state** capable of administering access to as well as defending and even extending the territories of the United States.

Conflict Over the Land Question

The early conflict over the land question and its connection with the issue of confederation prefigured the history of struggle between the North and South up to the Civil War. However, at the time of confederation the economic forces which were to give rise to distinct national formations in the North and South were only just beginning to develop.

Cotton production in the South in the 1780s amounted to no more than three thousand bales per year. The relative weakness of the slave agricultural economy was reflected in the near-adoption by Congress of a 1784 bill to prohibit slavery in the whole of the Public Domain.

Industrialization was also slow to develop. In the colonial period laws such as the Woolens Act, the Hat Act, the Iron Act, and the Navigation Acts had actually forbidden the manufacture and intercolonial trade of many finished commodities. The purpose of these laws was to preserve the colonies as sources of raw materials for English industry and as a market for finished products, such as clothing and tools, made in England. In the provincial period, independent merchants began to supply households in the Northeast with raw materials for domestic industry. By the late 1700s this

24 NATIONAL DEVELOPMENT OF THE NORTH AND SOUTH

putting-out system for woven products was quite widespread. Still, in 1789 the home market for goods was severely disjointed: only 3 percent of the population lived in cities, means of transportation between states were sorely lacking, and exchange was hampered by the chaotic condition of the currency. No national integration existed among these "united" states.

Capital formation based on **land speculation** promised to be the most direct route to laying the financial foundation for industrial development. Realizing this, land speculators in the North began seeking provisions allowing the sale of public lands to private parties (for resale at higher prices to small settlers). Also, following the peace with England the planters in the South turned their attention to expanding cotton production for trade with England. This revived the question of the status of slavery in the Public Domain.

To satisfy the immediate interests of both groupings two important ordinances were written. In the Ordinance of 1785 the federal government established a public lands policy which allowed the sale of large tracts of land to private concerns. Two years later the Northwest Ordinance clearly established the legality of slavery in the Public Domain south of the Ohio River. The legal basis for the westward movement of independent farmers and slave owners had been laid.

At the same time new developments in production and technology gave impetus to the process of national development in North America and foretold its divergence along separate lines in the North and South. The **cotton gin** was invented by Eli Whitney in 1793 and was later mass produced by David Pratt in Alabama. (Pratt and Whitney is now a leading jet engine manufacturer.) In 1797 the first **iron plows** manufactured in the Western Hemisphere were turned out by the newly emerging iron industry in the North. Plows were soon being mass produced in Pittsburgh and later in Chicago by new industrialists like John Deere.

Thus emerged the elements for separate economic development in agriculture. The durable iron plow was the basis for the westward expansion of small farmers in the North. The highly productive cotton gin paved the way for the expansion, also westward, of the slave-based cotton plantation system in the South. Ultimately, their struggle was joined in the Public Domain.

National Development of the South

The separate national development of the South began around 1793 with the invention of the cotton gin. National development before the Civil War consisted of two phases. The **first phase**, lasting until about 1830, resulted in the concentration of new cotton production in the Atlantic seaboard states, especially Virginia and South Carolina. The **second phase** involved the extension of cotton production into the Gulf states and the Mississippi River valley, especially Georgia, Alabama, west Tennessee, Mississippi, and Louisiana.

In the first year of operation for cotton gins, **cotton production** jumped from ten thousand to seventeen thousand bales. It climbed to an antebellum peak of 5.4 million bales in 1859. This level of production remained unsurpassed until after the defeat of Reconstruction in 1876. Figure 1 shows the tremendous importance of this commodity to the U.S. export economy between 1810 and 1870.

As production and international trade in cotton boomed before the war, so did the rise in river traffic from the plantation belt to thriving port cities on the coast. Excluding the Mississippi River and its tributaries, over five thousand miles of navigable rivers flowed into the Gulf of Mexico and another several thousand miles into the Atlantic Ocean.

The South thus developed one of the decisive characteristics of a nation—a **division of labor** between **town and country**. Although the **slave labor** which predominated on the cotton plantations in the countryside is not a form of labor typical of developed capitalism, slave-based agriculture formed the basis for capitalist industry in the towns and cities of the South.

Here is how William Gregg, a pioneer textile manufacturer in pre-war South Carolina, built capitalist industry in the midst of plantation slavery.

Figure 1

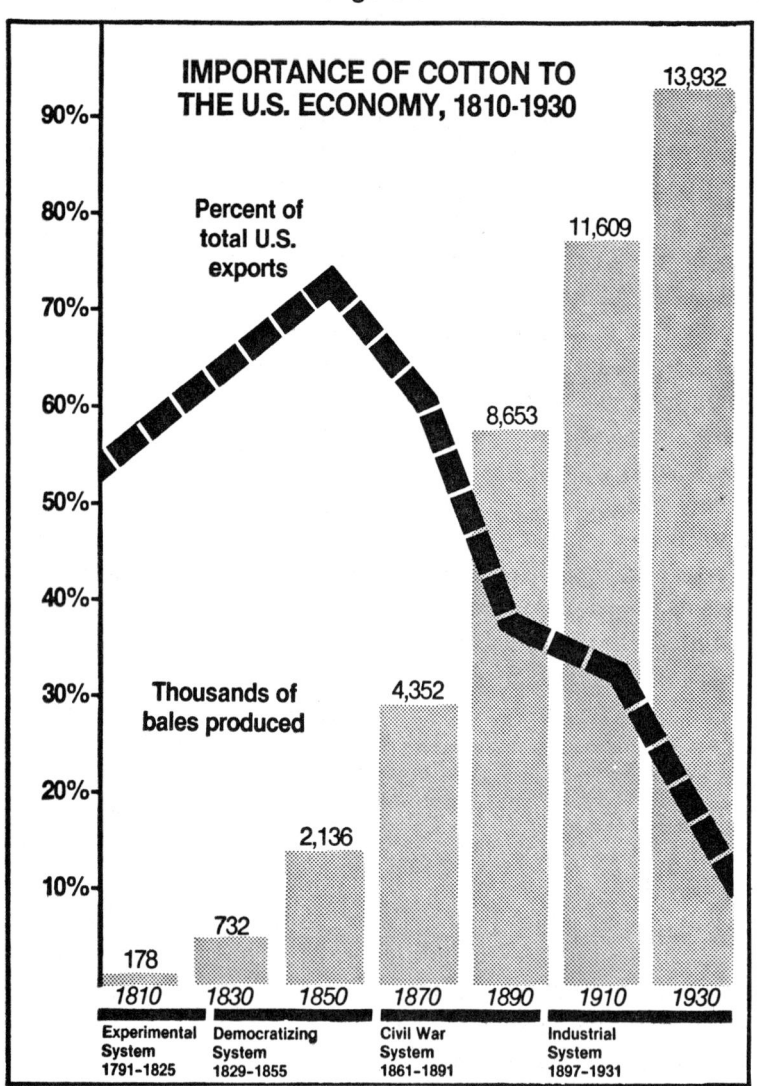

Source: **Historical Statistics of the United States, Colonial Times to 1970,** Series K-554, U-274, U-278.

[H]e wrote ten articles for the Charleston **Courier**, entitled "Essays on Domestic Industry," which were published in pamphlet form in 1845. In these essays he preached the new gospel of developing manufactures in the South by utilizing the great reservoir of poor white labor that had hitherto been largely neglected. He advocated confining slave labor to agriculture and to the reclamation of swamps.[3]

Gregg envisioned these new Southern mills entering into a kind of international competition with Northern mills.

The Southern mills, he thought, should at first confine their efforts to the production of the coarser cotton goods and should import experienced Northern men to aid in starting the factories. He pointed out that by building cotton mills the South could prevent the emigration of its sons to the West. Furthermore, he did not demand tariff protection for these infant industries, primarily because they specialized in making yarn and the cheaper grades of cloth, **which needed protection from New England** rather than from foreign nations.[4] [emphasis added]

Gregg built Graniteville Factory near the South Carolina-Georgia border not far from Augusta, Georgia and based the competitiveness of this operation on the wages paid to his workers.

The operatives were chiefly women and children over 12 years of age, for the older people who came from the hill districts and pine barrens did not have the flexibility to make good mill hands. The employees worked 12 hours a day, the men receiving four to five dollars a week, the women three to four dollars per week. The mill cottages rented from $16 to $25 a year. These wages were very low, but they compared favorably with agricultural wages in the South. It was an era when respectable, churchgoing factory owners both in the North and the South exploited human labor without recognizing any injustice in making large profits and giving their employees a pitiful share of the returns of their labor.[5]

The slave production of cotton generated the capital for the development of capitalist industry first in England, then in the North, and finally also in the South. Slave-produced cotton was a commodity for which no wages were paid. By selling this commodity on the world market, the capitalists accumulated the funds necessary to develop modern industry.

This assessment of slavery's role in the development of modern capitalism is also consistent with the later motion for the **abolition** of slavery. After the capitalist mode of production was set in motion and began accumulating capital on the basis of wage labor in industry, it was no longer necessary to accumulate capital on the basis of direct slavery.

Before the Civil War the South was producing 25 percent of the country's textiles and supplying the bulk of the world's cotton. Supporting this distinct Southern economy was an **infrastructure** separate from that of the North. In addition to the river transport system, the South built eight thousand miles of railroads in the 1850s, all based on a different gauge than in the North. These connected the plantation belt with the upland Piedmont and the commercial port cities of the coastal plain. Only three terminals linked the South with the North (Cairo, Louisville, and Baltimore).

The development of a **home** or **national market** for both agriculture and industry in the South closely paralleled this classic description of the rise of a national market.

> In fact, the events that transformed the small peasants into wage-laborers, and their means of subsistence and of labor into material elements of capital, created, at the same time, a home-market for the latter. Formerly, the peasant family produced the means of subsistence and the raw materials, which they themselves, for the most part, consumed. These raw materials and means of subsistence

have now become commodities; the larger farmer sells them, he finds his market in manufacturers. Yarn, linen, coarse woolen stuffs—things whose raw materials had been within the reach of every peasant family, had been spun and woven by it for its own use—were now transformed into articles of manufacture, to which the country districts at once served for markets. The many scattered customers, whom stray artisans until now had found in the numerous small producers working on their own account, concentrate themselves now into one great market provided for by industrial capital. Thus, hand in hand with the expropriation of the self-supporting peasants, with their separation from their means of production, goes the destruction of rural domestic industry, the process of separation between manufacture and agriculture. And only the destruction of rural domestic industry can give the internal market of a country that extension and consistence which the capitalist mode of production requires. ...Modern Industry alone, and finally, supplies, in machinery, the lasting basis of capitalist agriculture, expropriates radically the enormous majority of the agricultural population, and completes the separation between agriculture and rural domestic industry, whose roots—spinning and weaving—it tears up. It therefore also, for the first time, conquers for industrial capital the entire home market.[6]

In the South the development of a textile industry pulled the poor white dirt farmer off the land and into the factory for the first time. People who once produced homespun materials for their own use now provided the labor to manufacture textiles to supply the homes of the South. The textile industry provided a home market for raw cotton, and the cotton plantations provided a market for Southern-made machinery such as the cotton gin. The rivers and railroads tied together this national home market.

In describing the development of an actual national formation in the South, a further distinction must be made between the **core states** of the cotton and textile-producing South—that is, the coastal states from Virginia to east Texas—and the so-called **border states**. As one European war correspondent pointed out during the Civil War:

> None of the so-called border states, however, not even those in the possession of the Confederacy, were ever **actual slave states**. Rather, they constitute that area of the United States in which the system of slavery and the system of free labor exist side by side and contend for mastery....
>
> The chain of mountains that begins in Alabama and stretches northwards to the Hudson River—the spinal column, as it were, of the United States—cuts the so-called South into three parts.... The two lowlands sundered by the mountainous country, with their vast rice swamps and far-flung cotton plantations, are the actual area of slavery. The long wedge of mountainous country driven into the heart of slavery, with its correspondingly clear atmosphere, an invigorating climate and a soil rich in coal, salt, limestone, iron ore, gold, in short, every raw material necessary for a many-sided industrial development, is already for the most part a free country. In accordance with its physical constitution, the soil here can only be cultivated with success by free small farmers. Here the slave system vegetates only sporadically and never struck roots. In the largest part of the so-called border states, the dwellers on these highlands comprise the core of the free population, which in the interests of self-preservation already sides with the Northern party.[7]

The decisive blow by the Union Army against the Confederate States of America was launched from the mountainous region of east Tennessee. In speaking of a **Southern nation**, what is meant is the territory encompassing the plantation belt and the connected commercial and industrial centers on its fringe.

Southern Nationalism and Northern Secessionism

A number of classic historical works have dealt with the development of the Southern nation. Two important books in Louisiana State University's definitive "History of the South" series are Avery O. Craven's **The Growth of Southern Nationalism** and E. Merton Coulter's **The Confederate States of America**. A recent winner of the Allan Nevins Award of the Society of American Historians is John McCardell's **The Idea of a Southern Nation**.

Most focus on the political and ideological aspects of **Southern nationalism**. But the basis of this nationalism was economic, and it was constrained by the **basic economic law of slavery**.

> [C]ontinual expansion of territory and continual extension of slavery beyond their old limits is a law of life for the slave states of the Union.
>
> The cultivation of the Southern export articles, cotton, tobacco, sugar, etc., carried on by slaves, is only remunerative as long as it is conducted with large gangs of slaves, on a mass scale and on wide expanses of a naturally fertile soil, that requires only simple labor.... Even in South Carolina, where the slaves form four-sevenths of the population, the cultivation of cotton has for years been almost completely stationary in consequence of the exhaustion of the soil.... As soon as this point is reached, the acquisition of new territories becomes necessary, in order that one section of the slaveholders may equip new, fertile landed estates with slaves and in order that by this means a new market for slave-raising, therefore for the sale of slaves, may be created for the section left behind it.... In the Secessionist Congress at Montgomery, Senator Toombs, one of the spokesmen of the South, has strikingly formulated the economic law that commands the constant expansion of the territory of slavery. "In fifteen years more," said he, "without a great increase in slave territory, either the slaves

must be permitted to flee from the whites, or the whites must flee from the slaves."⁸

The political implications of this law were are follows:

> A strict confinement of slavery within its old terrain, therefore, was bound according to economic law to lead to its gradual effacement, in the political sphere to annihilate the hegemony that the slave states exercised through the Senate."⁹

The need for land dictated the **domestic policy** of the Southern nationalists on the proposed free-soil colonization of the Public Domain.

> [I]n order as far as possible to hinder the colonization of the Territories by free settlers, the slaveholders' party frustrated all the so-called free-soil measures, i.e., measures which were to secure to the settlers a definite amount of uncultivated state land free of charge.¹⁰

This naturally had a negative effect on poor whites in the South, who thus became a threat to the slaveholding system. Their allegiance to the Southern nationalists had to be held by other means, especially through **filibusters**.

> Finally, the number of actual slaveholders in the South of the Union does not amount to more than three hundred thousand, a narrow oligarchy that is confronted with many millions of so-called poor whites, whose numbers constantly grew through concentration of landed property.... Only by acquisition and the prospect of acquisition of **new** Territories, as well as by filibustering expeditions, is it possible to square the interests of these "poor whites" with those of the slaveholder, to give their turbulent longings for deeds a harmless direction and to tame them with the prospect of one day becoming slaveholders themselves.¹¹

Thus emerged the **foreign policy** of the Southern nationalists.

In the foreign, as in the domestic, policy of the United States, the interest of the slaveholders served as the guiding star. Buchanan had in fact purchased the office of President through the issue of the Ostend Manifesto, in which the acquisition of Cuba, whether by robbery or by force of arms, is proclaimed as the great task of national politics. Under his government northern Mexico was already divided among American land speculators, who impatiently awaited the signal to fall on Chihuahua, Coahuila and Sonora. The restless, piratical expeditions of the filibusterers against the states of Central America were directed no less from the White House at Washington.[12]

The South's first major move in its preparations for expansion came in 1803 and was conditioned by the ongoing struggle among nations on the European continent.

One of the consequences of the historic French Revolution of 1789 was the unleashing of a unified nationalist movement among the slaves and peasant farmers of the French colony of Haiti between 1790 and 1803. After a long struggle, Napoleon's forces were decisively defeated by a rebel army of fifty-five thousand (nearly three times the size of the army assembled by the Continental Congress for the revolutionary war against England). Thus, the French lost their key foothold in the Caribbean, from which they controlled their vast holdings known as Louisiana. Afterwards, France could only hope to prevent England, its main colonial rival, from gaining possession of this rich territory.

Ten thousand members of the deposed plantation-owning class fled from Haiti to the Southern ports of Charleston and New Orleans. These emigres injected into Southern politics an additional sense of urgency about consolidating control of the Gulf Coast against the threat of a slave insurrection backed up by the powerful Haitian army.

In those days Haiti's role in the Caribbean was similar to that of

Cuba today. Slaves throughout the hemisphere looked to Haiti as a model for their own futures.

Jefferson, the slave-owning President from Virginia, quickly concluded the Louisiana Purchase from France. By this act alone the territory of the United States was nearly doubled, and the richest agricultural region in the world came under federal control.

It was widely believed in the North that the Southern planters planned to carve a new block of slave states out of this territory and thus dominate Congress with pro-slavery senators and representatives. These concerns proved well-founded, for the South struggled mightily for the admission of several new slave states from this territory. The Missouri Compromise of 1820 and the 1854 Kansas-Nebraska Act were major legislative coups favoring the extension of slavery into the territory.

The immediate consequence of the Louisiana Purchase was the rise of a genuine **secessionist movement** in the North long before there was ever any secessionist movement in the South. This movement found expression in three successive incidents.

The first involved an attempt by political leaders in Massachusetts to unite the five New England states plus New York and New Jersey into an independent Northern Confederacy. This movement collapsed after the 1804 election, when the lame-duck vice-president of the United States, Aaron Burr, failed to win the governorship of New York, a key political post which the secessionists needed for organizing their movement.

The second secessionist effort also formed around Burr. This time it focused on the growing agricultural states and territories of the Ohio and Mississippi River valleys. Burr anticipated the necessity of wresting control of the Mississippi, its tributaries, and the port city of New Orleans from the Southern slaveholders or eventually falling under their sway. (This later became a Union strategy in the winning of the Civil War.) Burr's premature activities in the West ended in his arrest by the Jefferson administration in 1807 for treason. But because of the efforts of Chief Justice Marshall—the Southern President's arch-enemy on the Supreme Court—Burr was set free.

The third secessionist threat from the North involved mainly Massachusetts, Connecticut, and Rhode Island. It culminated in the Hartford Convention of 1814. The convention was called by New England merchants opposed to the South's expansionist policy toward Spanish Florida. This expansionism helped precipitate war with England (an ally of Spain) in 1812. The merchants were especially angered by the damage done to their commercial activity by the war at sea and because most of the war was fought along the northern border with Canada.

Secession was finally forestalled by the conclusion of a peace treaty with England, but the developing contradiction between the two national formations in the North and the South had been exposed.

National Development of the North

The early secessionist movements in the North arose in New England because New England was the focal point for the **first phase** of national development in the North. For years the economy there revolved around the carrying trade: cotton was imported from the South in exchange for foodstuffs and exported to England in exchange for manufactured goods. Only after the introduction of steam engines around 1830 did fully integrated textile operations begin to be conducted in New England. Thus, the **second phase** of national development in the North began about the same time as in the South.

The center of national development in both the North and the South soon shifted westward. European events created the conditions for this. The French Revolution, which led to the Louisiana Purchase, also presaged the wholesale expropriation of peasants from the land in northern Europe and their transformation into wage workers. One consequence of this process was a dramatic rise in **immigration** to the United States after 1830, especially from Ireland, Germany, and England. Before 1830, European immigration never exceeded one hundred thousand persons per decade, but in the three decades before the Civil War these figures reached

0.5 million, 1.6 million, and 2.5 million persons successively. Immigrants necessarily traveled the established routes of trans-Atlantic trade but generally tried to avoid landing in the South.

By 1860 the slave states had received only 500,000 immigrants and they accounted for only 13 percent of the nation's foreign-born. The South's major ports, Baltimore and New Orleans, attracted many of these foreigners, while the states of Maryland, Missouri, Louisiana, and Texas contained the majority of them. The Germans who were concentrated in Maryland, Missouri, and Texas, and the Irish, in Louisiana and Georgia, constituted most of the foreign-born population.

Most immigrants settled outside the South because they believed there were more opportunities in the free states. The newcomers did not want to compete with the plantation system and slave labor. Besides, by 1845 most of the best cotton land of the Old South had been gobbled up by planters.[13]

These trends ultimately led to the South losing control of the **House of Representatives**.

Immigrants who landed in New York and Boston moved westward along the route opened up by the Erie Canal in 1825. They provided most of the labor for the expansion of the canal system in the North up to 1850 and for railroad construction thereafter. These two systems served as the basic **infrastructure** of the North before the Civil War and connected the Great Lakes basin with the Northeast. Canal and railroad workers settled in Cleveland, Detroit, and Chicago as wage laborers. Others with a thirst for land farmed the countryside and plains beyond.

The rise of cereal and hog production in the Midwest sustained the growth of these cities. The number of cities with over eight thousand residents climbed from 13 in 1820 to 141 in 1860. In turn, the cities of the North produced more and more manufactured goods for the majority of the population still on the land.

Pittsburgh turned out thirty-four thousand iron plows per year in the 1830s. In Massachusetts plow manufacture climbed from sixty-one thousand in 1845 to one hundred fifty-three thousand just ten years later. By 1860 Chicago was manufacturing four thousand reaping machines per year for use on the Great Plains. The development of a **home market** for both agriculture and industry—united by an extensive infrastructure—marked the maturing of the **town and country division of labor** of the national formation in the North.

Northern Nationalism and Southern Secessionism

As territories in the North reached certain legally defined population levels they became eligible for admission to the United States as states. Gradually the Southern nation's political domination of the federation and its economic policies began to be threatened by the burgeoning power of the Northern nation. In 1816, 1824, and 1828 the North utilized its growing power in Congress to legislate increasingly higher **tariffs** on commodity imports in order to protect its new industries from European competition. The South sold most of its cotton to England and preferred free trade so it could use its English pounds to buy English goods as cheaply as possible. When the tariff was raised a fourth time in 1832, talk of Southern **secession** arose in South Carolina, whose economy was one of the most heavily tied to slave production of cotton for trade with England.

However, President Jackson and other southern slaveholders were not convinced that the South had to pull out of the federation in order to maintain its political and economic integrity. They secured a compromise reduction in the tariffs which South Carolina had threatened to "nullify" unilaterally. At the same time they redoubled their efforts to bring new slave states into the United States in accord with the provisions of the Missouri Compromise of 1820.

An important effort to annex new territory below Missouri's southern border began with the provoked secession of Texas from

Mexico in 1836. Originally, Texas was entitled to form as many as five states out of its territory. The addition of five more slave states would have given the South control of the Senate in compensation for its minority position in the House. But by 1845 the immigrant German population in Texas was so large that any plan to divide up the state would have backfired and created more free states than slave states because of the free-soil sympathies of the immigrant farmers. Thus the whole of Texas was admitted as the last slave state in 1845. The forces underlying the growth of the Northern nation were now directly undermining the expansion of slavery in the Southwest and therefore threatening the existence of the slave economy of the Southern nation.

In 1846 President Polk and other representatives of the slaveholders provoked a two-year war with Mexico. Having despoiled Mexico of its northern lands but unable to immediately carve any more slave states out of this territory, the South turned its attention to the cultivatible areas of Central America and the Caribbean. An imposter government headed by a Southerner was established in Nicaragua. The U.S. ambassador to England, James Buchanan, proposed that the United States also issue an ultimatum (the Ostend Manifesto) to Spain that it sell Cuba to the United States or the United States would seize it by force. However, the puppet government in Nicaragua was ousted by an alliance of Central American states, and the Pierce administration rejected the Ostend Manifesto as premature. (Cuba was later seized from Spain in 1898.) Finally, with the admission of five more free states from the Northwest and West after 1846, the Southern nation's hopes to control the **Senate** dissolved.

Buchanan's proposed manifesto won him the 1856 Democratic presidential nomination. In addition to Southern Democrats, his supporters included some Northerners who favored the extension of slavery in order to expand the flow of cheap cotton to eastern mills. In a three-way race, Whig candidate Millard Fillmore split the vote that otherwise would have gone to the new Republican Party, and Buchanan won the presidency.

By 1860, however, the growing working class in the North was falling firmly in line behind the free labor policies of the Republican Party, the new party of industry. This party developed out of a relief organization formed in the Midwest in the 1850s. It supplied farmers in the Kansas territory with men, arms, and money to fight Southern guerrillas who were attempting to take over the territory and bring it into the Union as a slave state. However, the Republican Party was not for the **abolition** of slavery. It was simply against the further extension of slavery in the territories of the United States.

Sentiment in the North was in favor of keeping these lands open and available to small farmer-settlers. This policy ultimately found a following among some Democrats in the North and split the Democratic organization there. Nonetheless, the two Democratic tickets in the 1860 election had platform planks calling for the acquisition of Cuba and strict enforcement of the Fugitive Slave Act of 1850. This time the split among the Democrats allowed the Republicans to capture the House, the Senate, and Presidency.

The Southern nation's last foothold in the federal state apparatus was the **judiciary**. In the Dred Scott decision of 1857 the Supreme Court had declared unconstitutional all previous legislative restrictions on the expansion of slavery. The economic system of the North could no more tolerate this decision than the South could politically enforce it.

The course toward secession was set. Upon Lincoln's election—and with lame duck President Buchanan still commander-in-chief of the armed forces and able to block any mobilization of federal troops—the slaveholders moved quickly to constitute the Southern nation as a separate nation-state, the Confederate States of America.

Some political forces in Europe counseled the North to accept the existence of two North American republics as an historical inevitability. But both nations understood perfectly well that their contradictory interests made further coexistence and mutual expansion of their market systems impossible. On both sides the drive for capital translated into a drive for territory at each other's expense. Thus, the long struggle for the consolidation of the Public

Domain within the economic system of either nation ended in the decisive **Civil War** for the political domination of North America.

[T]he war of the Southern Confederacy is in the true sense of the word a war of conquest for the extension and perpetuation of slavery. The greater part of the border states and Territories are still in the possession of the Union, whose side they have taken first through the ballot-box and then with arms. The Confederacy, however, counts them for the "South" and seeks to conquer them from the Union. In the border states which the Confederacy has occupied for the time being, it holds the relatively free highlands in check by martial law. Within the actual slave states themselves it supplants the hitherto existing democracy by the unrestricted oligarchy of three hundred thousand slaveholders.

With the relinquishment of its plans of conquest the Southern Confederacy would relinquish its capacity to live and the purpose of secession. Secession, indeed, only took place because within the Union the transformation of the border states and Territories into slave states seemed no longer attainable. On the other hand, with a peaceful cession of the contested territory to the Southern Confederacy the North would surrender to the slave republic more than three-quarters of the entire territory of the United States. The North would lose the Gulf of Mexico altogether, the Atlantic Ocean from Pensacola Bay to Delaware Bay and would even cut itself off from the Pacific Ocean. Missouri, Kansas, New Mexico, Arkansas and Texas would draw California after them. Incapable of wresting the mouth of the Mississippi from the hands of the strong, hostile slave republic in the South, the great agricultural states in the basin between the Rocky Mountains and the Alleghenies, in the valleys of the Mississippi, the Missouri and the Ohio, would be compelled by their economic interests to secede from the North and enter the Southern Confederacy. These northwestern states, in their turn, would draw after them all the Northern states lying further east, with perhaps the exception of the states of New England, into the same vortex of secession.

Thus there would in fact take place, not a dissolution of the Union, but a **reorganization** of it, a **reorganization on the basis of slavery**, under the recognized control of the slaveholding oligarchy. The plan of such a reorganization has been openly proclaimed by the principal speakers of the South at the Congress of Montgomery and explains the paragraph of the new Constitution which leaves it open to every state of the old Union to join the new Confederacy. The slave system would infect the whole Union. In the Northern states, where Negro slavery is in practice unworkable, the white working class would gradually be forced down to the level of helotry. This would accord with the loudly proclaimed principle that only certain races are capable of freedom, and as the actual labor is the lot of the Negro in the South, so in the North it is the lot of the German and the Irishman, or their direct descendants.

The present struggle between the North and South is, therefore, nothing but a struggle between two social systems, between the system of slavery and the system of free labor. The struggle has broken out because the two systems can no longer live peacefully side by side on the North American continent. It can only be ended by the victory of one system or the other.[14]

Thus began the war between the North and South.

The Colonization of the South

The Civil War resulted in the conquest of the Southern Confederacy by the Northern Union. Hundreds of books have been written about the military strategies and campaigns of this war. Much of this information is revealing about the root cause and objectives of the war simply because war is an extension of politics and politics an extension of economics. But comparable in interest to the military campaigns is the war-time **economic legislation**.

The Republican Party—a minority party when it won the 1860 election because of the split in the Democratic Party—took full advantage of its political victory and legislated an economiç program which became the foundation for the next seventy years of economic development in the United States.

> [Republicans] were neither Abolitionists nor egalitarians: the unequal status of Negroes and poor southern whites was of no interest to them. But, as spokesmen for industrial capitalism, the war furnished them the opportunity to round out the **economic** program of the class which they represented. Industrial capitalism was now in control of the state and they used it for the following purposes: 1. A vast extension of the credit base of the nation took place (as a result of bond flotations and greenback issues) and these resources were used to build up industrial capitalism via the route of war contracts. 2. The tax scheme was heavily weighted against the small consumers through a ramified program of indirect taxation, again aiding accumulation. 3. A protective tariff was written. 4. A national banking system was devised. 5. A Pacific railway was chartered which was not only given generous grants from the public domain but also lent federal funds. 6. A homestead law was passed. 7. Appropriations for internal improvements—river and harbor legislation—were made. 8. The admission of immigrant contract labor was authorized. 9. The military was employed to put down strikes.[15]

This was a program comparable in scope to the Hamiltonian legislation of the late 1700s, the Jeffersonian-Jacksonian program of the early 1800s, the progressive reforms of the 1890s, New Deal legislation in the 1930s, and "Reaganomics" in the 1980s.

The impact of these policies was not confined to the North.

They wanted to maintain the South in vassalage, too....
In short, as conscious and clear-eyed spokesmen for the triumphant industrial-capitalist class, they saw that the South was an important element in establishing a vast domestic market and a functioning capitalist economy. Southern products—cotton, tobacco, sugar, turpentine, lumber, hemp—were needed at home and to help balance international payments abroad. Southern raw material—iron, coal—could be exploited by the investment of northern capital surpluses. Southern railroads could be built, factories erected, cities furnished with public utilities—always provided the section was prepared to co-operate with northern capital.[16]

With the Southern nation's economy stripped of capital as a result of war costs and physically devastated by the scorched-earth campaigns of the Northern armies, Southern capital was in no position to maintain control of its **home market**. With the assistance of Reconstruction governments, occupying armies, and military governors—all of which were regarded as temporary political devices to help attain economic objectives—the penetration of Northern capital into the South began.

Here is one famous Southern sociologist's analysis of the substance of **Southern colonization**.

[A] colonial economy is a debtor economy. It begins as an investment on the part of the mother country; it accumulates little capital of its own; it lacks the organization of credit, and as economic opportunities arise on the frontier, they must be financed from outside the area. The surplus returns are exported as profits and interest to outside business men in command of capital. Thus the South has often turned the development of her basic resources—forestry, coal, iron, petroleum, and minerals—over to outside interests at rock bottom prices—all for lack of credit with which to finance development. The South capitalized its labor force under slavery, thus constricting its credit resources. The rise of textiles was largely financed by northern machinery manufacturers and commission merchants.... The South has been in the position of exporting leaders to the nation, importing investments, and exporting to other areas the dividends from this colonial economy.[17]

The colonization of the South began in the **plantation economy**.

To say that plantations of a sort were preserved and enlarged is not to say that the antebellum planter was preserved also. The antebellum planter of Louisiana whose plantation remained in his family after 1880 was rather the exception than the rule. In the Sugar Bowl there was a veritable "revolution in land titles" resulting increasingly in a "new, capitalistic sugar aristocracy, organized in corporations and financed by banks"; and "At least half the planters after 1870 were either Northern men or were supported by Northern money." F.C. Morehead, President of the National Cotton Planters' Association, estimated in 1881 that not one third of the cotton plantations of the Mississippi Valley were "owned by the men who held them at the end of the war," and that others were daily passing "into the hands of the commission merchants" at that time.[18]

Control also extended into **industry** and the **infrastructure**.

As the old century drew to a close and the new century progressed through the first decade, the penetration of the South by Northeastern capital continued at an accelerated pace. The Morgans, Mellons, and Rockefellers sent their agents to take charge of the region's railroads, mines, furnaces, and financial corporations, and eventually of many of its distributive institutions. Southern counterparts of the Northeastern masters, however, failed to appear. The number of Southern businessmen increased steadily, and some of them waxed in fortune. But the new men, as well as many of the old, acted as agents, retainers, and executives—rarely as principals. The economy over which they presided was increasingly coming to be one of branch plants, branch banks, captive mines, and chain stores.[19]

The new tempo of industrialization which began with World War II only solidified the South's dependent status.

[There was] a growing public unrest over the South's tributary status, its undeveloped potentialities, its "colonial economy"—a phrase increasingly current. Events of the Depression years had exposed the raw-material economy to violent fluctuations and had underscored the uses of even sweatshop industries in raising incomes. But the drive for industry raised another dilemma. The quest for capital and branch plants led inevitably to the imperial North, and thus to outside control and to the drain of profits and interest from the region.[20]

The colonized status of the South grew out of the aftermath of the Civil War. Since then, its national economy has been integrated into a multi-national system controlled by industry and finance in the North. In what way, then, has the South survived as a nation?

What fundamentally distinguishes one national market from another is the differential operation of wage-labor markets. From the beginning of the plantation economy to modern industrialization today, the South has continued to represent a separate **national labor market** within the multi-national system of the United States. Because of slavery the value of wage labor was depressed in the South compared to the North, and since the Civil War Northern capital has taken full advantage of—and consciously perpetuated—this fundamental national characteristic of the South. For example, here is a description of why Northern capital was being invested in the South in the late 1800s and early 1900s.

Among the advantages debated or conceded were the South's newer machinery, cheaper labor, lower taxes, proximity to raw materials, cheap water power, milder climate —the list grew with the controversy and was enlarged upon by Southern boomers and capital seekers. In a spirit of candor, however, the **Manufacturers' Record** advised New England to seek the real explanation in the answer to the question "why England is shipping textile machinery to India and other parts of the East." Edwin L. Godkin, who viewed economics from the standpoint of empire, made the same comparison: "The condition of the Massachusetts mills," he observed, "finds its parallel in England. The greatest market for British cotton is India, but cotton spinning in India has been advancing slowly during the same time and by the same means that the industry has been growing in the Carolinas. Nearness to the raw material, which the India spinner enjoys, is the smallest part of his advantage. Here too, the wage question is the great factor. Wages of the Indian operative are only ten to twenty cents per day, and the hours of labor are such as the employer chooses to make."

Dismissing the South's other advantages as of minor importance, a committee of the influential Arkwright Club of New England came to the following conclusion: "We have, therefore, practically only to consider the problem that is presented by the fact that labor is cheaper in the South; that the hours of labor are longer, and that there is neither any of the restrictive legislation urged among us by the labor unions, and very generally placed upon our statute-books, nor any prospect even of an early agitation in behalf of such restrictions. . . . So far as we could learn there is no disposition to organize labor unions." The report estimated that the cost of labor was 40 per cent lower in the South than in New England, and that the working day in North Carolina was 24 per cent longer than in Massachusetts.[21]

With the movement of capital southward, the industrial demand

THE COLONIZATION OF THE SOUTH 47

for labor has necessarily raised the value of labor in the South. But Northern policy makers have explicitly regulated the value of Southern labor in order to maintain an advantageous **wage differential** between the Northern and Southern labor markets. For example, the following has been pointed out about the National Recovery Act passed during the 1930s depression.

> Actually, a clause in the recovery act permitted differentials "according to the locality of employment" and in about half the codes businessmen included variant wage minimums according to geographical or population differences. Among the forty-six codes covering "manufacturing products," eleven set lower minimums for the South.[22]

In the rush to industrialize the South following World War II, the Taft-Hartley Act of 1947 played a key role in maintaining different wage scales in the North and the South. Capital considered this especially important since in 1946 the AFL-CIO had launched its "Operation Dixie" campaign to organize Southern labor.[23] To maintain the North-South differential, the bill originally introduced by Representative Fred Hartley, Jr. (Rep.-N.J.) and later co-sponsored by Senator Robert Taft (Rep.-Ohio) proposed "ban[ning] industry-wide bargaining in a comparatively simple fashion." Here Representative Hartley goes on to explain the logic behind this objective.

> In many industries labor costs are the largest factor in arriving at sale prices for products. Industry-wide bargaining on wages thereby removes differing wage costs from the area of competition and, in effect, stifles competition in that industry.[24]

The final Taft-Hartley Act achieved this objective with the infamous Section 14(b), which makes it legal for states to implement union-restricting **right-to-work laws**. As a result, industry-wide bargaining has indeed been restricted on a territorial basis.

Two years later, there were ten "right-to-work" states; by 1954 there were 16; and by 1963 there were 19. In 1976, Louisiana, the only Southern state without this criminal law, tragically entered the "right-to-work" column.

The "right-to-work" laws became the main legal road block the capitalists rely upon to keep the Southern worker "in his place" and prevent the unionization of the South.

It is for this very reason that companies that operate in the South make a higher rate of profit.[25]

The impact on workers in the same industry but on different sides of the North-South border is striking.

While Akron Goodyear workers average $5.50 per hour, Tennessee rubber workers average $3.89 per hour; Virginians, $4.16; and Mississippians, $3.90.

G.M. has recently opened six new plants in Mississippi, Georgia, Alabama and Louisiana. These workers are affected by "right-to-work" laws and receive anywhere from $2 to $3 per hour less than Northern workers doing the same jobs, while receiving less benefits.[26]

Thus the South has become the industrial heartland of "right-to-work" legislation, and the basically non-union wages of the South clearly differentiate the labor market there from the heavily unionized one in the North (Figure 2).

This is not simply a matter of **racial discrimination**.

How does the theory of "racism" explain why a black worker in the North is paid more than **either** a black or white worker in the South; why, while the northern white operative makes six percent more than the northern black, he makes 71 percent more than the southern black; why a southern white operative makes 22 percent less than a northern black operative? How does it explain why, while the southern white operative makes 32 percent more than the southern

FIGURE 2
NORTH-SOUTH INCOME DIFFERENTIAL, 1974
(Mean Income for Two-Income Families)

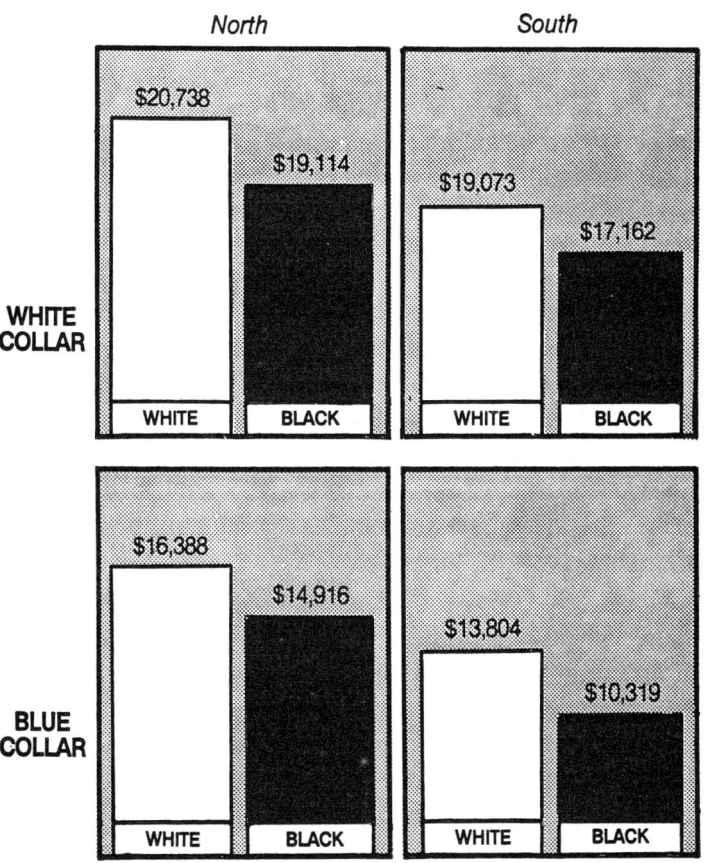

Source: **Statistical Abstract of the United States, 1977**, Table 721.

black operative, the northern black operative makes 62 percent more than the southern black operative? Why the North-South differential which transcends "race"?[27]

The answer is found in the **colonized status** of the South. The Southern nation has been a colony of the North since the end of the Civil War. There has, of course, been a certain interpenetration of the two national economies and markets since then. But this is true of all modern nations and does not negate their separate national identities. Economic integration and trade are no more indicative of the disappearance of national boundaries than is the lack of trade an essential attribute of national differentiation.

The case of Puerto Rico is the clearest example of this rule. The Puerto Rican economy is highly integrated with that of the United States. Yet Puerto Rico still is widely recognized within the United Nations as a distinct nation—a **colonized nation** within the multinational system of the United States.

The South is essentially no different. The North has consciously enforced labor market differences in the South, thus perpetuating the basis for all other national distinctions between North and South. This is characteristic of **multi-national states** in general, and in particular of the two main English-derived systems in North America—the United States and Canada.

3.

The South as an Economic Reserve

Almost everyone in the North and South who can trace their family back to the Civil War has a story to tell about that conflict. I have the chess set that a distant relative—a colonel in the cavalry—carried in a small wooden box in his saddlebags throughout the war. My wife has the last two letters received from a relative still warmly referred to in family circles as "Uncle Tommy." He died on 5 May 1864 in the Battle of the Wilderness, the opening contest in a month of battles that were the bloodiest of the whole war.

Grant had hoped to get through the Wilderness into clear country before giving battle; but wagon trains delayed his movements, and on the 5th and 6th, in dense thickets where orderly battle plans were impossible, the two armies came to grips in a series of engagements so complicated that any description in terms of corps and divisions is impracticable in these pages. Union losses approximated 18,000, of whom over 2000 were killed; the Confederate loss probably exceeded 10,000. . . .

In the fighting from May 5 to May 12, much of which was hand-to-hand, Grant is said to have lost over 26,000 in killed and wounded. Yet with grim resolve to fight it out on that line "if it . . . [took] all summer," he pushed on to Cold Harbor,

52 THE SOUTH AS AN ECONOMIC RESERVE

where he brought on the severest fighting moments of the war and committed a costly error. With Lee's army squarely blocking the way behind strong intrenchments, Grant hurled three corps against an enfilading fire of the enemy (June 3, 1864), losing more men in the eight minutes of hottest fighting than in any similar period in the war. The 12,000 killed and wounded in this attack produced a shudder in the North, intensified the peace movement and the opposition to Lincoln, and created in Union ranks an impression of reckless insanity in their commander combined with a suicidal willingness to follow. Facing their death in obedience to fatal orders, many of the men had written their names and addresses on strips of paper and pinned them to their coats for the identification of their dead bodies.

In the whole campaign from the Wilderness to Cold Harbor, the Union losses were approximately 55,000, nearly as much as Lee's whole army.[1]

The North's losses were human losses and hence temporary because of the North's greater manpower reserves. For the South the results of the war were much more disastrous and enduring.

The war brought widespread devastation to the South. Conquering troops tore up the main rail lines to disrupt Confederate troop and supply movements. Those lines which were not completely destroyed fell into disrepair because there was no one to maintain them. The banks which funded the Confederate war effort went bankrupt and their currency became worthless. Without finances and with all the free white labor called to arms, industrial production collapsed. The slave population at the heart of the Southern economy opened a "second front." Left relatively unguarded as the free population went to the military front, the slaves initiated a mass **general strike** in the fields across the South. As a result, in 1864 cotton production dropped to its lowest level in forty-six years.[2]

Conquered and colonized by the North, the Southern nation constituted an immense potential source of raw materials and relatively inexpensive labor. After the Civil War, one would expect that money would have poured into the South to take advantage of these economic factors. It was not that simple.

The North fought the war to rid itself of political domination by the South, to capture full control of the federal government, and to implement an economic program suitable to industrial expansion. An immense outpouring of resources to reconstruct Southern infrastructures would have been necessary before industrializing the South. The North, on the other hand, suffered relatively minor physical damage as a result of Confederate army incursions early in the war. Its first priority was full-scale **industrialization** on its home ground.

The South's desperate economic situation is well illustrated by the story of how the mouth of the Mississippi River was reopened to navigation. Without adequate manpower and equipment to dredge the delta during the war, the mouth of the river became clogged with mud. It was impassible to river traffic and therefore a serious hindrance to the rebuilding of normal economic life in the lower Mississippi valley. The main impediment to rectifying this situation was the Northern-controlled federal government, which had no immediate interest in reopening the river and so refused adequate funding or support for such a project.

> In 1876 Captain James B. Eads, the famous engineer, won the acclaim of a hero from the Delta people by freeing the mouth of their river from the control, not of Spaniard, English, or French, but of mud. By Herculean labors and inexpensive methods he had constructed jetties of willow mattress that turned the current and cut through the mud bars blocking the mouth of the river a channel deep enough to admit ocean-going vessels of deep draft into the port of New Orleans.[3]

Because of its subordinate status the South was forced to go to such lengths to accomplish anything independently of the North. The South had become a colony of the North—an **economic** reserve subject to easy exploitation. U.S. history shows that only under certain conditions has Northern capital taken advantage of this reserve. This periodic development of the South has been a major source of strength in helping capital endure its own crises.

The Theory of Political-Economic Realignment

The key to understanding the periodic influx of capital into the South lies in understanding the dynamics of **political-economic realignment** in U.S. history. In Chapter One, nations were defined as the political-economic formation (i.e., the form of society) which accompanied the rise of capitalist methods of production. Underlying the development of nations was the invention of **machinery**, which made industrial production on the basis of wage labor possible for the first time in history.

Once a nation has developed and based its economy on a certain set of industries, those industries tend to dominate the economy for at least several decades. This does not mean, however, that they do not experience crises. Every technical advance in those industries tends to result in **crises of overproduction**.

> The extension of the markets cannot keep pace with the extension of production. The collision becomes inevitable, and as this cannot produce any real solution so long as it does not break in pieces the capitalist mode of production, the collisions become periodic. Capitalist production has begotten another "vicious circle.". . .
>
> [C]ommerce is at a standstill, the markets are glutted, products accumulate, as multitudinous as they are unsaleable, hard cash disappears, credit vanishes, factories are closed, the mass of the workers are in want of the means of subsistence, because they have produced too much of the means of subsistence; bankruptcy follows upon bankruptcy, execution upon execution. The stagnation lasts for years; productive forces and products are wasted and destroyed

wholesale, until the accumulated mass of commodities finally filters off, more or less depreciated in value, until production and exchange gradually begin to move again. Little by little the pace quickens. It becomes a trot. The industrial trot breaks into a canter, the canter in turn grows into the headlong gallop of a perfect steeplechase of industry, commercial credit, and speculation which finally, after breakneck leaps, ends where it began—in the ditch of a crisis. And so over and over again.[4]

This is a good description of the **business cycle** in capitalist countries. These cycles are inexorably linked with the dynamics of capitalist production itself. With the industrial revolution of the early 1800s, capitalism "for the first time open[ed] the periodic cycle of its modern life."[5]

The first major industry in the Western capitalist countries was the textile industry. Because this industry was supplied with cotton mainly from the South, **slavery** was the economic and social foundation of the modern industrial era.

Direct slavery is just as much the pivot of bourgeois industry as machinery, credits, etc. Without slavery you have no cotton; without cotton you have no modern industry. It is slavery that has given the colonies their value; it is the colonies that have created world trade, and it is world trade that is the pre-condition of large-scale industry.[6]

Of course, slavery was abolished in North America, and the textile industry is no longer the heart of the economic system of any Western nation.

What accounts for the changing **structural composition** of the economy? During certain **critical economic crises**, national specialization in a system of old industries is superseded by specialization in a system of new industries.

Sectors which, in recent decades, have been expanding at an accelerated pace are often called new, while sectors which develop more slowly are designated as old. These names are largely true. As a rule, the faster growing sectors have appeared later than the slower growing and, drawing on the advantages of technological progress, they are actively competing with the old.[7]

These structural changes are further based on the utilization of new technologies and new sources of energy. One industrial marketing consultant writing in **High Technology** magazine has summed this up.

> In the 1920s, the Soviet economist Nikolai D. Kondratieff suggested that, with respect to wholesale prices, the world economy followed cycles lasting from 50-60 years. Other economists subsequently tied these price cycles to the business cycle and to waves of technological advance. Thus, boom periods are associated with the exploitation of technology that has reached an advanced state of commercialization. These are also times of rising prices. The ensuing cycle troughs are linked to minimal investment and underutilized capacity. In order to start the world economy moving again, the backlog of innovative technology that accumulates during boom times must be implemented.[8]

Thus critical crises find their resolution in the rapid development of new industrial sectors based on new technologies. Diverting investment into these newer sectors causes the economy to undergo structural change. An **economic realignment** occurs, and the life of a political-economic formation enters a new period of development. However, the **social basis for production** remains unchanged. In the case of nations, production continues to be carried out on the basis of the relationship between **wage labor** and **capital**.

Insofar as politics is the concentrated expression of economics, every economic realignment has its political parallel. Critical crises bring about not only an economic realignment but also a **political realignment** within the framework of the particular class structure.

The development of the means of production constantly changes not only the social systems as epochs of human history, but within epochs it generates a complex struggle within the ruling class based upon the fact that the development of the productive forces constantly gives one or another section of that class control of a decisive form of wealth. . . .
As Marx noted in **Capital**, the wealth of bourgeois society presents itself as an immense accumulation of commodities. But at any given time the control of a particular form of that wealth has acted as a decisive lever for a section of the bourgeoisie in the struggle for political hegemony. . . .
A shifting of political balance must necessarily ensue, as with every other shift in control of the decisive form of wealth. The struggle between the newcomers and the grouping that controlled political power on the basis of a previously decisive form of wealth is bound to bring about a destabilization and, as with every struggle within the ruling class, it is bound to create the conditions for a revolutionary upsurge on the part of the workers.[9]

There have been a number of **revolutionary upsurges** in the country's history. A revolutionary upsurge among workers and a **political split** within the capitalist class are the two main factors distinguishing one **political-economic period** from another.

Economic Realignments in U.S. History

There have been literally dozens of recessions and depressions of different lengths and depths in U.S. history (Appendix A). Only a few resulted in political-economic realignment.

In the early stages of U.S. history there were almost no industries in the country because mercantile acts passed by the English crown forbade the production and export of such basic commodities as wool, hats, molasses, iron, and sugar. Most capital invested in economic activity went into the shipping and **carrying**

FIGURE 3
MAJOR FORMS OF CAPITAL IN DIFFERENT PARTY SYSTEM PERIODS
Percent of total capital

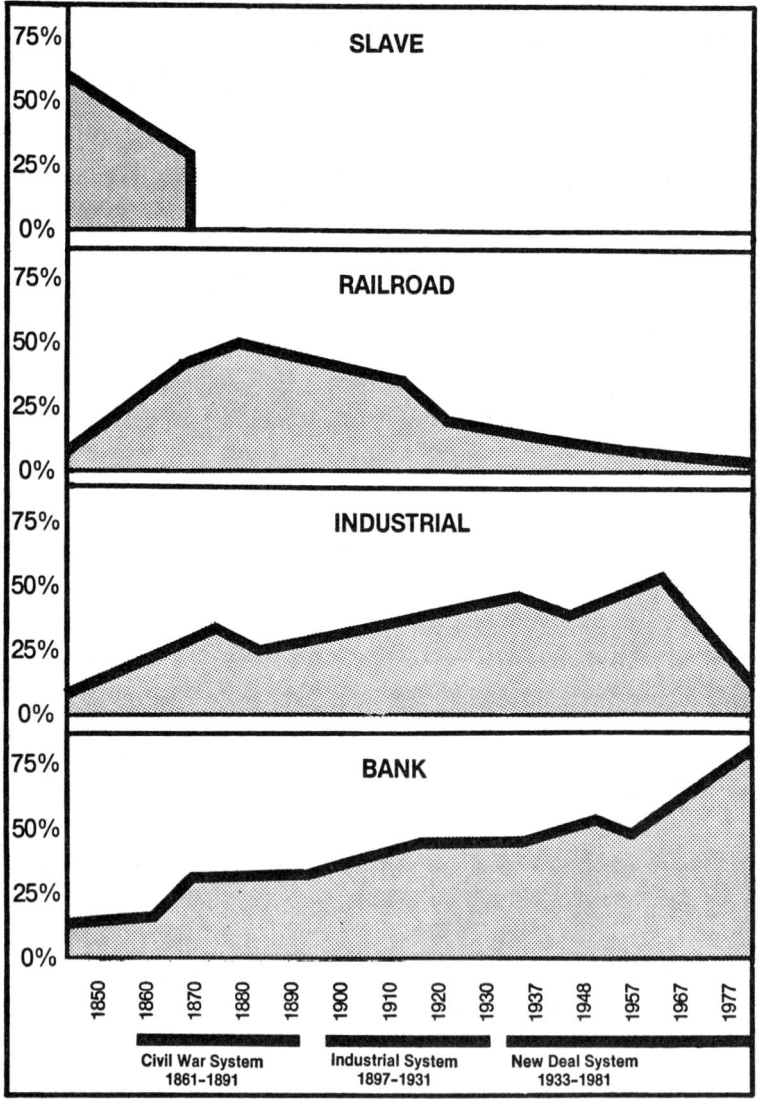

Source: Appendix B, p. 170

trade. After independence, a major agricultural industry finally developed in North America—the **cotton industry**. The main areas of investment in this industry were in land and slaves. With the Emancipation Proclamation of 1863, the capital invested in slaves was effectively obliterated (Figure 3).

Prior to the Civil War and abolition, new industries were developing (especially textiles and an infant iron industry which formed the base of the emerging railroad system). The capital invested in **railroads** (including land and equipment) was greater than the capital invested in all **manufacturing industries** combined. This relationship between the railroads and industry persisted for a long time after the Civil War, although eventually the book value of all manufacturing industries surpassed that of the railroads.

Meanwhile, **banks** were investing in all kinds of productive ventures including the cotton industry, railroad transport, and manufacturing. As the banks earned profits from these investments, the owners of banks began to control more assets than the owners of all industries and railroads combined.

The shift in the balance of power between these main sectors of the economy can be gauged by comparing the historical changes in total **capital investments** in each (Figure 3). In the first half of the 1800s the capital in slave labor consistently outweighed the total capital in railroads, industries, and banks. The Civil War marked an economic turning point. By 1870 railroad capital was greater than either industrial capital or total banks assets; combined railroad and industrial capital easily overwhelmed bank assets. Just before World War I, however, industrial capital began to pull even with railroad capital. World War I marked another economic turning point. By 1919 industrial capital was almost double the value of railroad capital. The new open hearth steel industry continued to produce steel for the still expanding railroad system, and together railroad and manufacturing capital outdistanced bank assets for awhile longer. Then World War II brought another turning point as bank assets climbed above total capital invested in railroads and manufacturing. By 1973 commercial bank assets alone were more than double the total capital in railroads and industry.

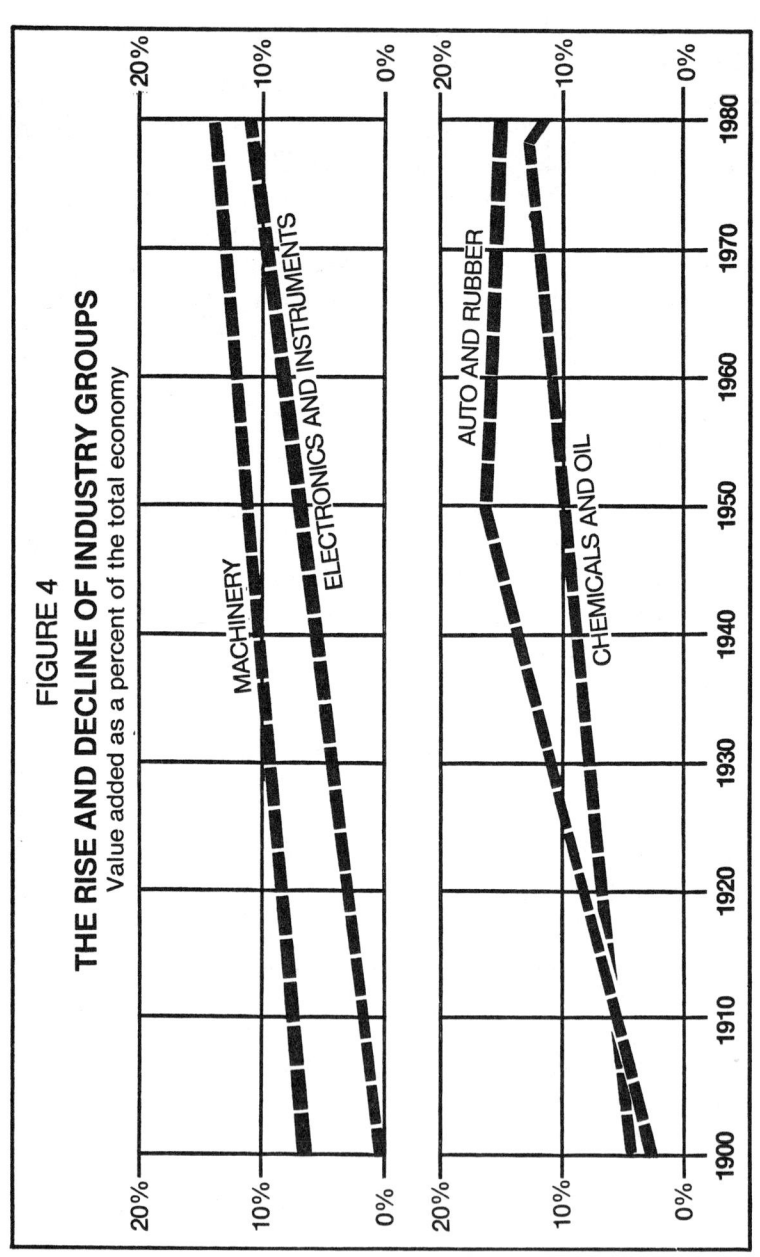

FIGURE 4
THE RISE AND DECLINE OF INDUSTRY GROUPS
Value added as a percent of the total economy

ECONOMIC REALIGNMENTS IN U. S. HISTORY 61

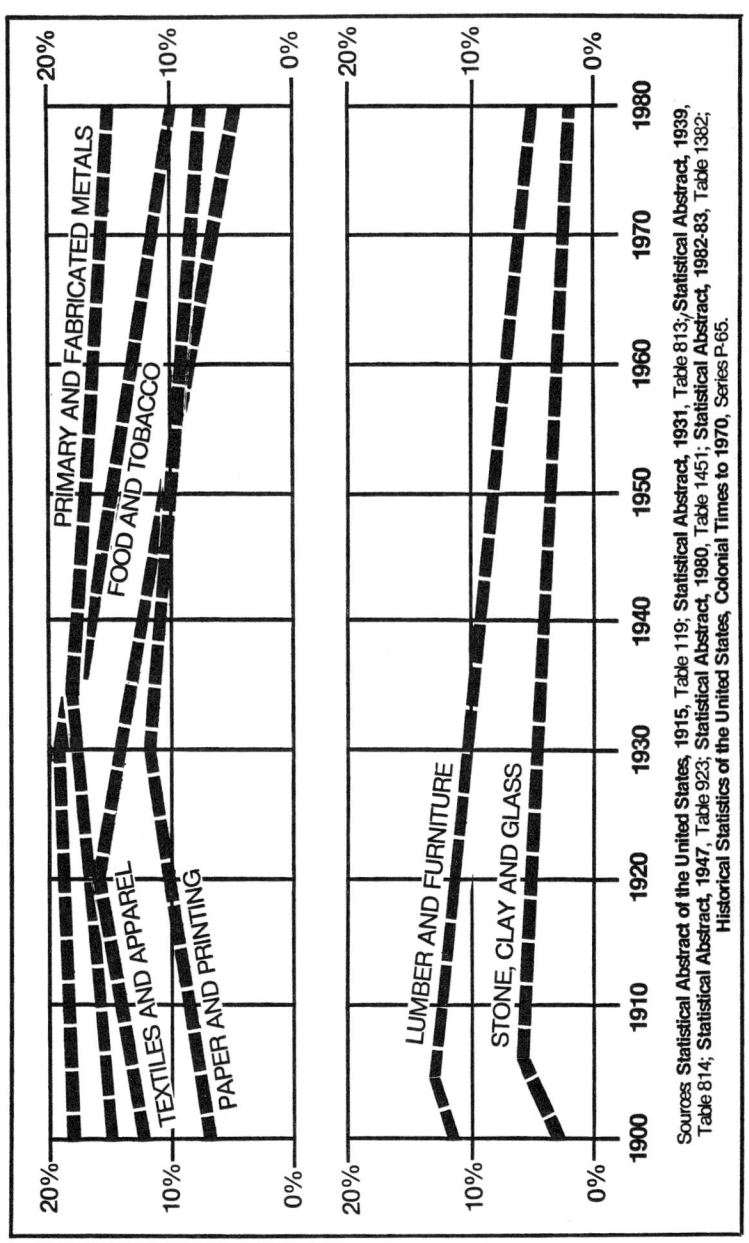

Sources: **Statistical Abstract of the United States,** 1915, Table 119; **Statistical Abstract,** 1931, Table 813; **Statistical Abstract,** 1939, Table 814; **Statistical Abstract,** 1947, Table 923; **Statistical Abstract,** 1980, Table 1451; **Statistical Abstract,** 1982-83, Table 1382; **Historical Statistics of the United States, Colonial Times to 1970,** Series P-65.

62 THE SOUTH AS AN ECONOMIC RESERVE

This analysis of shifts in the importance of main sectors of the economy pinpoints five major **economic periods** in U.S. history. The carrying trade was the prevalent economic activity in the late 1700s and reached its peak of prosperity around 1830.[10] Then slave-based cotton production became the chief area of economic activity until the Civil War. From the Civil War to World War I, railroad capital dominated industrial capital; between the two world wars this relationship was reversed. Throughout both periods, combined railroad and industrial capital exceeded all bank assets. Since World War II, the center of balance for capital has shifted solidly to the banks, especially to commercial banks.

The fact that banks have gained the ascendancy in the economy does not mean that the economy has become a **financial economy** as opposed to an **industrial economy**. Banks are incapable of directly producing commodities. In the early days of the country when a banker would enter a joint venture with an independently wealthy industrialist, the industrialist's investment usually outweighed that of the banker. Accordingly, the industrialist retained the most say in the way production was organized and carried out. As bank capital grew, this relationship began to change. In the 1870s the "practice now emerged of bankers demanding a share in management control before granting credit... although the general practice was not conspicuous until the 1890's."[11] Today banks hold the upper hand in management decisions wherever their investments are concerned (for example, in refurbishing the Chrysler Corporation, rescheduling New York City's municipal debt, and refinancing the debts of neocolonies.[12]

Through their investments banks remain strongly linked to industry and its course of development. Thus the economic changes in the country should also be reflected in key **industrial periods**. A compilation of data shows this. Figure 4 covers 1899 to 1980 and shows trends in the proportion of value produced by leading industries. It presents a picture of the rise and fall in importance of various industries in modern U.S. history.

In each new economic period particular industries rose to dominate the economy. The **critical crises** of the 1890s, 1930s and 1980s mark transition points in the structure of the economy. As a result of the crisis of the 1890s, the leather, lumber, and furniture and stone, clay, and glass industries peaked. In the crisis of 1920-21, the textile and apparel industries also peaked. Meanwhile the paper and printing, food and tobacco, and primary and fabricated metal industries were on the rise. They all peaked during the critical crisis of 1929-33 or the subsequent crisis of 1937-38. Industries rising after the 1930s were auto, rubber, chemicals, and oil. Auto and rubber reached a plateau following the 1953-54 crisis, but have declined sharply as a result of the crisis of the 1980s. Chemicals and oil climbed in importance over the same period but hit a plateau following the oil crisis of 1973-75. The only industries which have been rising sharply in recent years are electronics, instruments, and the machinery industry, the latter having been reorganized on the basis of **high technology** with its most promising sector being computer machinery. Computers and electronics represent the best prospects for the reorganization of the economy on another industrial basis. This is precisely where investment capital is flowing today.

Political Realignments in U.S. History

These economic periods are reflected in **political periods**. The theory of political periods in U.S. history is one that political scientists have been developing in recent times.

Among the central revelations of American political analysis in the post-World War II period has been the discovery, primarily through the relatively new instrument of survey research, of remarkably stable patterns of partisan loyalty.... Upon this stability was predicated the concept of the "normal" vote, the customary partisan distribution of the vote in the absence of unusual external forces.... This pattern in turn suggested the construction of a threefold typology of partisan elections: maintaining, deviating, and realigning.... The third type of election, relatively rare but of major impact, is the **realigning** election, in which popular ex-

64 THE SOUTH AS AN ECONOMIC RESERVE

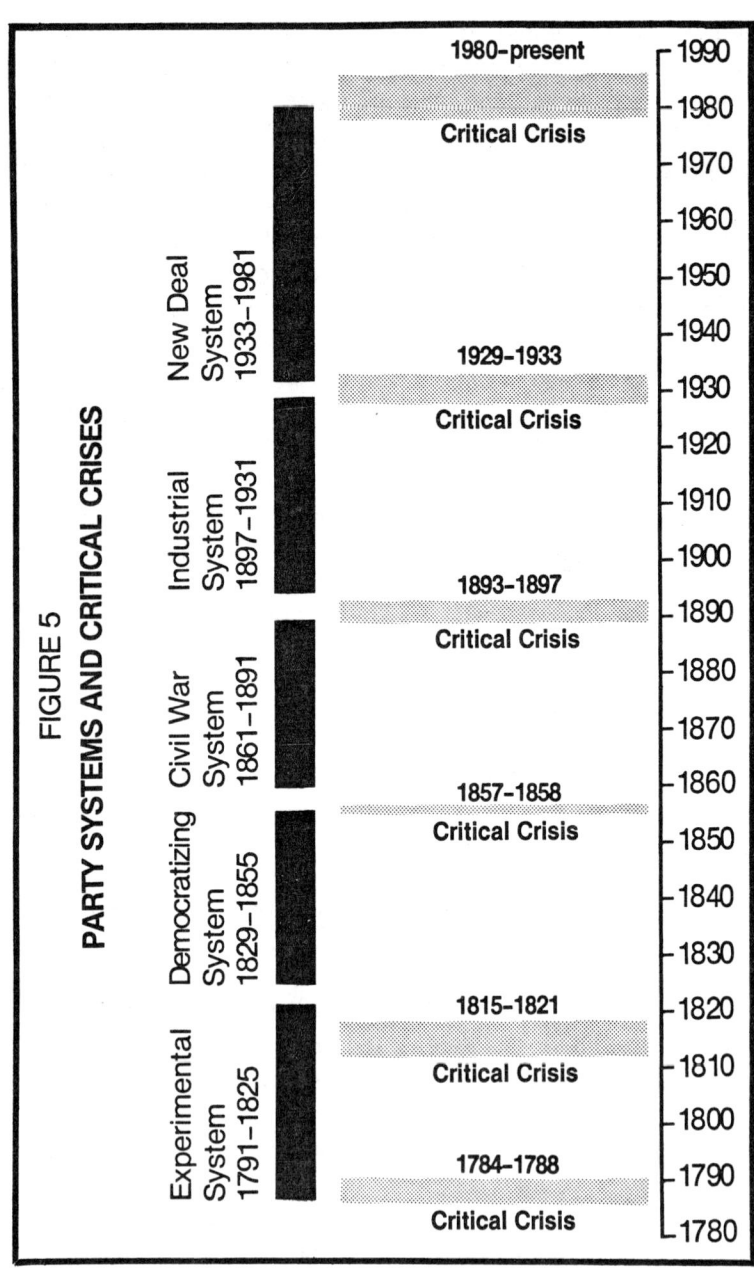

FIGURE 5
PARTY SYSTEMS AND CRITICAL CRISES

citement associated with politics is sufficiently intense and durable to basically transform the electorate's loyalties and thereby create a new "normal" partisan majority. Both political scientists and historians have recently employed the model of critical realignment to reconstruct our understanding of the entire evolution of American political life, focusing less on ephemeral candidates and issues and even on individual parties than on party systems, of which, by rough consensus, there have been five.[13]

These five **party systems** are the Experimental System (c. 1791-1825), the Democratizing System (c. 1829-1855), the Civil War System (c. 1861-1891), the Industrial System (c. 1897-1931), and the New Deal System (c. 1933-1981). These are shown in Figure 5. Between these systems are years of transition in which the old dominant political parties lose their influence among the population and other parties are formed or revived to take their place. Every new party system, its politicians, and their policies reflect the new economic realities of each period.

The early economy of the United States revolved around the merchant marine, an industry which went into decline after 1830. This focus on trade and related questions of tariffs and duties necessarily placed foreign relations at the top of the list of policy issues for every administration in this period. Thus, a contradiction between the mercantilist North (led by the Federalist Party) and the agarian South and West (represented by the Democratic-Republicans) characterized the first party system in U.S. history.

The first of these was the **Experimental System**, lasting from 1789 to roughly 1824. Despite the Founders' theoretical opposition to "divisive faction," and to some extent precisely because of this initial denial of legitimacy to the concept of party, the Federalists and the Republicans clashed bitterly, especially over foreign policy and its domestic implications, and thereby foreshadowed the bimodal partisanship that was to take its modern form after 1824.[14] [emphasis added]

The second economic period began with the decline of the merchant marine and the rapid growth of slave capital. There was a corresponding political realignment at the beginning of this economic period, characterized by the rise of both the Jacksonian Democrats and the opposition Whig Party. The **Democratizing Party System** emerged.

The Democratizing System, during the period 1828 to 1854, centered on a democratized presidency and attendant patronage, and both Jacksonian Democrats and Whigs demonstrated extraordinarily creative organizational innovations to mobilize mass participation.... Then, as the system matured, the new Whig opposition came to accept the policy and organizational implications of white manhood suffrage, especially after the Jacksonians attempted to dismantle the neo-mercantilist federal structure they had inherited from the Founders.[15]

A key issue in this period was the struggle to replace the old political system designed to serve a mercantilist, trading economy with a new system designed to promote new economic interests. This was the period in which the political struggle between the planters in the Southern nation and the free-soilers and rising industrialists in the Northern nation came to a head. In this struggle over economic issues, the Democratizing System inevitably disintegrated and gave rise to a new system corresponding to the economic period lasting from the Civil War to the depression of the 1890s. During this period railroad capital was predominant.

As northern Whigs flirted with Free-Soilers, Whiggery became highly suspect in the South, and when the Kansas-Nebraska Act of 1854 overturned the old modalities of compromise that had permitted the anti-slavery and free-soil controversies to be papered over, the Whigs disintegrated....

The deterioration of party structure during the 1850s foreshadowed the emergence of the **Civil War System** of

1860-92. The increasingly turbulent national politics drove a traditionalist and entrenched but obsessively fearful southern elite to take desperate measures in response to both real and imaginary threats to the political, economic, and racial status quo. During the Civil War, the new Republican government, suddenly enjoying enormous artificial majorities in Congress, not only delivered the **coup de grace** to slavery but also launched a neo-Whiggish, positive federal program in banking, currency, transportation, tariff, and land-grant policy. This radical transformation had been largely consolidated by the early 1870s.[16] [first emphasis added]

This party structure foundered on the rocks of the Populist movement of the 1890s, a movement largely centered in the colonized Southern nation and directed against Northern control. The basis for this revolt is clearly shown in this description of railroad **freight-rate differentials** enforced between North and South.

The Interstate Commerce Commission recognized the connection between industrial development and freight-rate differentials as early as 1889. In an opinion concerning a case from the South, the Commission held freight-rate inequalities "in a very great degree responsible for the lack of local development in that region, except at favored localities."

Justifying their policy on the grounds of low population density, seasonal fluctuations, low-grade cargo, and the predominance of one-way and local traffic, the Southern carriers had from the beginning charged higher rates per mile than Northern carriers. The distinctive Southern freight rates and classifications were institutionalized on a regional basis in the seventies and eighties by railway associations and pools that established "boundaries more tangible than the Confederacy ever achieved," with a capital in Atlanta and a rate sovereignty extending from the Chesapeake to the Gulf. After 1887 the Interstate Commerce Commission gave legal sanction to the railway-association rates and classifications and recognized a "Southern Territory" with boundaries running along the Ohio and Potomac and dipping into Virginia on the north and following the Mississippi on the west. Similarly, an "Official Territory" north of the Ohio and east of the Mississippi, and a "Southwestern Territory" including Arkansas, Louisiana, Texas and a slice of New Mexico, as well as two other western rate territories were evolved and recognized.

Certain trade advantages accrued from these rate differentials. Since a little over half of the population and considerably more than half of the wealth and buying power of the country was located in Official Territory, that region became a powerful magnet for goods. It was a market in which all manufacturers of a national scale had to compete. Manufacturers within the favored region moved their products much greater distances for an equal amount of money than could those in outlying territories. Nor did the barriers operate reciprocally, for Official Territory shippers could penetrate into the Southern market at a somewhat lower rate, mile for mile, than their competitors in the South had to pay for shipping similar articles wholly within their own territory. "Thus, one had here something remarkably similar to the working of a protective tariff, to the extent that certain favored interests effectively strive to protect themselves at home while retaining privileges elsewhere."[17]

That is a good description of just one of the main methods of control exerted by **Northern imperialism** over its **Southern colony**. And this was the political consequence.

Hence the third party system grew increasingly unstable as two disadvantaged strata, the cash-crop farmers of the economically colonialized South and West and the ethnically fragmented urban proletariat, grew increasingly restive under the two conservative-dominated major parties.... [T]he

Populist party of the 1890s mushroomed in the wake of the "Democratic" Depression of 1893 to attempt the truly formidable task of forging a biracial and multi-ethnic alliance of the rural and urban dispossessed.

The abortive Populist revolt combined with the depression of the 1890s as an important contributing factor to the evolution of the fourth party system, the **Industrial System** of 1894-1932.[18] [emphasis added]

A widespread nationalist counter-reaction among Northerners against this Southern nationalism strengthened the hand of the Republican Party and especially its "progressive" industrial wing, which took over the reins of power from the old "robber baron" railroad wing.

The massive Democratic defections during the 1890s in the greater Northeast created a reliably Republican bastion that effectively controlled a system which served to insulate the dominant industrial elites from the victims of the industrializing process, despite the protesting political movements repeatedly launched from the quasi-colonial West.[19]

However:

[T]he normal Republican majority... abruptly disintegrated following the crash of 1929.
The **New Deal System**, forged during the critical realignment period of 1928-36, rested upon a dominant coalition formed from such an unlikely amalgam of constituent voting blocs as the Solid South, blacks, organized labor, urban ethnic groups, disgruntled farmers, and liberal intellectuals.[20] [emphasis added]

The New Deal coalition included the solid bloc of conservative Southern Democrats. This party system held together in various forms through the Carter administration of 1977-1981. Now this period appears to be at an end economically and therefore politically.

Only recently political hegemony shifted from the hands of those who controlled industry into the hands of those who controlled money. We are now living through another dramatic change.[21]

Today the capitalist market cannot expand because the capitalist system cannot expand. Consequently production must continue to decline. The revolutionization of the means of production constantly lowers the rate of profit and gluts the market. The frantic effort to maintain maximum profits in the face of this revolutionization is seen in the scramble by the most influential groupings of international financiers to maintain their control of wealth by moving away from the glutted energy sector and attempting to control high technology. The result is a sharp struggle between the energy and the technology sectors of the bourgeoisie, a development favorable to the politicization of the workers.[22]

The rise of the "New Right" and the passage in 1981 of the most conservative economic legislation in a long time are the political reflections of the decay of an old economic alignment and the concerted effort by the **smokestack industries** to protect their troubled position against the plan for high technology **reindustrialization**. This plan is described in a special report by Nelson Rockefeller to President Nixon about the **re-division of labor** within the Western Hemisphere.

What is needed now is a broadening division of labor among the nations of the Western Hemisphere. At present, the United States is producing, at high cost behind tariff walls and quotas, goods which could be produced more economically by other hemisphere nations. The U.S. is short of skilled labor and, if anything, this shortage promises to get worse. The shortage of skilled labor is intensified when the U.S. continues to keep workers in lines which are, by definition, inefficient, since production can only be carried on here behind tariff or quota barriers. National productivity would be enhanced by shifting workers and capital out of protected industries into industries where advanced technology and intensive capital investment permit the U.S. to pay high wages and still remain competitive in world markets. The goods the United States is now producing inefficiently would be imported, mainly from less developed countries. Consumers would gain through lower prices, workers would receive higher wages, and the return on capital would be higher.

The less developed countries would also gain. With abundant supplies of labor and wage levels well below those in the United States, they could export processed foods, textiles, apparel, footwear, and other light manufactures, as well as meat and other farm products. This would provide increased employment at higher wages than are now available. Workers could move off farms into higher paid industrial jobs. The increase in income would raise living standards generally, contributing to the improvement in the quality of life. **Such nations would become better customers for the high-technology products of the United States.**[23] [emphasis added]

The details of this proposal are the basis for the reindustrialization policy of the leading Wall Street banks and what **Business Week** magazine has described as the "Atari" Democrats. There has been only one significant modification: the steel and auto industries are also shifting more and more into the less-developed countries of the hemisphere.[24]

The Rockefeller proposal is entirely consistent with the fact that the main new industry developed in the United States during the past two decades has been the **computer machinery** industry, which is based in the **semiconductor electronics** industry. The United States dominates world production of computers, and this new technology is becoming central to every advance in manufacturing and assembly techniques, office systems, and military hardware. Indeed:

> [I]n 10 years' time, industry forecasters expect semiconductors, with sales of more than $90 billion, to be one of the world's largest industries. This business will also be the platform on which two of the world's four largest industries in 1990 will be built—computers and telecommunications.[25]

Crises, Wars, and the Realignment Cycle

This analysis of political-economic realignments in the United States began by identifying general periods in which merchant capital, slave capital, railroad capital, industrial capital, and bank capital were economically dominant. It then identified corresponding political periods in terms of party systems: Experimental, Democratizing, Civil War, Industrial, and New Deal.

Each of these political-economic periods is checkered with numerous recessions and depressions (Appendix A). These crises may be designated as **intermediate crises** so long as there is room for the fuller development of the leading economic sector of the period. But some crises must be designated as **critical crises**, the proverbial "straw that breaks the camel's back," because they force the transition to a new political-economic alignment. Critical crises occurred in 1784-1788, 1815-1821, 1857-1858, 1893-1897, and 1929-1933. The character of every critical crisis reflects both the declining and rising economic sectors and results in political destabilization. The economic crisis which began in 1980 has all the earmarks of becoming another such critical crisis.

Critical crises are merely the first step in a **realignment cycle**. Subsequent steps include the winning of **state power** by the representatives of the rising sector of the economy, the passage of an **economic program** appropriate to the fullest development of that sector, intermediate crises during expansion, and the conducting of wars as engines for the recovery of the economy and for enhancing the international position of the new economic sector. These intermediate crises and wars therefore also reflect the character of each particular period.

In the colonial period English merchants controlled North American trade. But the crisis beginning in 1772 showed the emerging merchant class among the colonialists that they had little future so long as they were tied to English capital.

> The British banking crisis of the summer, with the ensuing credit contraction, brought widespread inventory liquidation and distress to colonial importers.[26]

The **War for Independence** followed in 1776. A peace treaty was signed in 1783, but the confederation of former colonies as yet had no functioning central government or party system representing North American economic interests. The **critical crisis of 1784-1788** changed all that.

> Indeed, it may be argued plausibly... that merchants—particularly in the import trade—and land speculators... using temporary financial and business recession as a pretext and political uncertainty as a weapon, sought to entrench themselves once and for all in the seats of government through the establishment of a powerful national union.[27]

Three years later—in 1791—the party system of government developed for the first time. It has continued to this day.

The Experimental Party System period was marked by the predominance of the mercantilist economic policies of Alexander Hamilton. These policies remained in force throughout the Jeffersonian "Era of Good Feelings." There were three intermediate crises in this period due mainly to excessive importations of British goods or the collapse of European export markets. Either way, U.S. merchants were hurt. The period is also noted for five wars, four of which involved disputes about international trade and commerce with France, the Barbary States, England, and Algiers (Appendix C).

The **critical crisis of 1815-1821** effectively ended this period and introduced a new period of political-economic alignment. After the War of 1812:

> Resumption of importations hurt U.S. manufacturing, but the down-trend was checked by European demand for American farm staples. As farm commodities soared and bank credit was liberalized, a wave of land speculation occurred. However with the collapse of foreign markets prices broke in the fall (1819), land values sank rapidly, and numerous banks and mercantile houses failed in the **1st major banking crisis** in U.S. history, with general business depressed until 1822.[28]

This crisis began as a **trade speculation** crisis but touched off a land speculation crisis. It therefore also revealed the central issue of economic development which would characterize the next period—agricultural expansion in the South and West.

The period was also marked by three intermediate crises, the largest of which occurred from 1837 to 1843 and clearly reflected the economic trends of the times.

> The crisis of 1837... was one of the many series of crops of tares that land speculation sowed. In the years immediately preceding the panic, every public land office became an exchange thronged with milling dealers who bought pre-emption claims, soldier lands, and government sections and who often paid for them in the "rag money" of the wildcat banks.[29]
>
> The collapse in real estate was followed in the 2nd quarter of 1837 by a precipitate fall in stock and commodity prices and an acute banking crisis....
>
> The decline was briefly halted in 1838 as business activity appeared to be building toward a secondary boom, but a ma-

jor break came in 1839 when the Bank of the U.S., now a Pennsylvania-chartered bank, closed its doors after an unsuccessful attempt to sustain cotton prices. The crisis was followed by a protracted depression, with its low point near February 1843.[30]

This intermediate crisis set the stage for the **Mexican-American War**, the capture of new lands, and the intensification of land speculation. The war was most actively pursued by the South, which expected to gain new lands for the expansion of cotton production and slavery in New Mexico (the upper Rio Grande Valley), Arizona (the lower Colorado River Valley), and California (the Central Valley). But it also served the plans of emerging Northern railroad interests who envisioned a southern route to the Pacific Ocean over this territory. Two Indian wars in the period also secured new lands in the South and Midwest (Appendix C).

The **critical crisis of 1857-1858** spelled the end of an economy based on **land speculation**, cotton expansion, and slavery.

The 1850's saw the speculative land mania reaching its final heights. There was one break in the trade following the recession of 1851; then in 1854 the fever chart began to mount again until, in 1857, it was estimated, more than $800,000,000 was invested in land deals. When the crash came in 1857—a crash that had world-wide repercussions—it shook not merely the jerry-built edifice of the speculators but the whole structure of mercantile capitalism as well. Vast paper fortunes were made in land speculation; and sizable real sums were lost in it....

It is significant to note that no outstanding merchant-capitalist fortune emerged out of wild land speculation. By the late 1850's, American capitalism had learned this very important lesson.[31]

It is also significant that during this crisis "some of the larger western railroads went into bankruptcy"[32] for the first time, thus providing an indication of which new economic powers were coming to the foreground.

The **Civil War** was fought early in the next period and served primarily as an engine to reshape the political economy of the country. The subsequent period of Indian Wars in the West brutally cleared the way for the extension of the railroads to the West Coast. This was the period of the robber barons who accumulated huge tracts of public land at no cost. The rails were laid across this land mostly by immigrant Irish and Chinese labor. With a front on the Pacific, import/export trade with Asia became feasible. The United States began to extend its military hegemony into the Pacific. Puppet regimes were established in Samoa and Hawaii, and Japan and China were forced to open their doors to trade.

But even the railroads were not invincible. Periodically they lapsed into crises, and ultimately they succumbed to the growing power of manufactures. In the period of the Civil War Party System there were four intermediate crises, the most severe occurring in 1873-1878.

> The feverish industrial and agricultural activity in the north during the Civil War, aided by the rising prices, had inaugurated a period of unprecedented prosperity. Immense regions in the west had been opened up to agriculture, while the easy profits of war prosperity had been invested freely in fixed forms of capital, notably transportation facilities. The prosperity had been too rapid, the expenditures too lavish, to be healthy; and the decade of the seventies opened with underlying conditions far from encouraging. Enormous amounts of capital had been sunk in railroads to finance the 30,000 miles built between 1867 and 1873, from which small immediate returns could be expected. The opening of western lands had thrown the older areas out of cultivation and decreased their value. Speculation and extravagance were rampant, and the business morality of politicians and capitalists, as witnessed by the Credit Mobilier and the Black Friday scandals, left much to be desired. The failure in

September, 1873, of the country's leading brokerage firm, Jay Cooke & Company, then engaged in building the Northern Pacific Railroad, precipitated the most severe panic up to that time in our history.[33]

The consequences revealed the extent of **railroad speculation** in the economy.

In 1872, out of three hundred and sixty-four listed rail securities, only one hundred and four were paying dividends. They moved into insolvency when hard-pressed foreign investors wanted cash.

It was no accident that the American banking house most closely linked with European capital—Jay Cooke and Company of Philadelphia and New York—should crack first. Its New York office closed its doors in September, 1873, and brokerage houses began to tumble. Railroad bankruptcies followed, the exchanges shut down, and commercial failures mounted sharply. Before 1873 was over, 5000 such failures were reported, involving liabilities of $228,000,000. As for the rails, eighty-nine were in default on bond issues worth $400,000,000. The depression continued for six years: railroad building virtually stopped; the unemployed reached at one time 3,000,000; immigration slowed up; prices dropped by 30 percent below the level of 1870-73; there were wide-spread vagrancy and serious industrial conflict.[34]

But there was still room left for the expansion of the economy on this basis. By 1883 new track construction reached well over eleven thousand miles per year, and old iron track began to be replaced with steel rails. Finally, heavier locomotives and cars were also moved into operation over the new rails, and the steel industry boomed.

The **critical crisis of 1893-1897** dealt a death blow to the predominance of railroad capital. However, it also wrought havoc in the growing industrial sector.

The failure of the Philadelphia and Reading Railroad in February and the National Cordage Company in May ushered in the panic of 1893. Many banks all over the country suspended business; an increasing number of commercial and industrial failures followed; a stock market panic occurred; the gold reserve of the government fell below the accepted minimum of $100,000,000; business was demoralized. The Erie, Northern Pacific, the Union Pacific, and other railroads followed the Philadelphia and Reading into bankruptcy until one-fourth of the railroad capital was in receivership. In the first year of the panic there were more than 15,000 business failures with liabilities amounting to $437,000,000. During the same year, 158 national banks, and several hundred state and private banks closed their doors. Securities fell in value; the dividends of companies that survived were cut or omitted; factories were shut down; committees were organized in the cities to provide food and relief for large numbers of unemployed.[35]

The new industrial period was ushered in on the wings of **reform**: that is, the old trusts and monopolies from the previous period were reformed by "progressives" in the Republican Party. The depression of the 1890s wiped out weaker companies and concentrated their resources more and more in the hands of new monopolies favored by the progressives. The revamped Republicans had labor in their pocket because of these reforms and because of the new prosperity of the period.

An important part of the basis for growth was the opening of new international markets for U.S. industry as a result of the **Spanish-American War**.

[T]he rapid concentration of capital and consolidation of business which has been a marked feature of our economic life since 1898 has aided in financial imperialism. An industrial organization of the size and power of the Standard Oil or a banking concern of the importance of the National

City Bank with resources of over a billion, is obviously in a better position than a small company to push its interests in foreign fields, in competition with European investors.[36]

The impact of **World War I** also brought a change in the international influence of U.S. capital.

The tremendous cost of carrying on the war forced the withdrawal of much European capital invested abroad, thus leaving the field open to our own financiers. By the end of the conflict we had not only taken over many European holdings in other countries, but had loaned heavily in Europe. Before the war the British were the chief investors in "foreign" fields, with almost twenty billion dollars loaned in the international markets as compared with nine billions for France and six for Germany. At the conclusion of the war the foreign investments of Great Britain and France had decreased to but a fraction of their former amounts, while Germany had been practically eliminated. On the other hand, the United States found herself the leading investing nation of the world, with nine and a half billion dollars loaned to the allied nations, other foreign investments amounting to eight billions, and with notice loans and goods on consignment amounting to several billions more.

Overnight, as it were, we became the great creditor nation, and the interests this position implies [would] ultimately be reflected in changes in both domestic and foreign policies.[37]

On the North American continent this was the period in which capitalists claimed that "what is good for General Motors is good for the country" (and also for Canada, where branch plants were rapidly being established). It was also a period of unprecedented war and military intervention by the U.S. government, especially in the Caribbean and Central America but also in Asia, Europe, and even the Soviet Union (Appendix C).

Besides being a period of expansion, it was a period of persistent crises related to that expansion. The industrial character of the period is clearly seen in the numerous crises arising from **stock market speculation**, as reflected in the newly introduced Dow Jones Industrial Average. Thus in 1907:

> Some of the new trust companies were deeply involved in stock market manipulations. The panic started with a stock market break and the consequent failure of one of the most vulnerable trust companies. Other failures followed in rapid succession.[38]

The wars of the period had their own special impact on the economy, again reflected most sharply in stocks and industry.

The outbreak of the conflict in Europe in 1914 resulted in a collapse of the financial markets of the world, which were unprepared for the coming of war. The London Stock Exchange, in an unprecedented move, closed on July 31. European investors had already begun to convert their American securities into cash, and as wholesale liquidation of American stocks and bonds was threatened, the New York Stock Exchange also suspended on the same day. The stock exchanges all over the country, likewise, closed their doors. Not until December 12 was the New York Stock Exchange opened for limited trading. In April, 1915, unrestricted trading was permitted.[39]

Then after the war:

> After reaching a peak in May, 1920, commodity prices declined and business began to slow down. Retail dealers, who had high-priced goods on their shelves, and manufacturers, who had costly raw materials on hand, were in a serious predicament. Banks contracted loans; railroad freight loadings and earnings declined; and factories closed down. By the spring of 1921 over four million persons were unemployed.[40]

The worst was saved for last. After the 1920-1921 recession:

> A rising tide of prosperity was sustained by conspicuous expansion of the consumers' durable goods industry. A boom in construction and real estate also developed (Florida real estate boom collapsed in 1926). By 1927 residential construction, auto output, purchases of consumers' durable goods, and new investment in producers' durable goods had begun to decline; but the boom continued, fed almost entirely by **unprecedented securities speculation not reflected in commodity prices**.... The spectacular crash of stock prices occurred in Oct.-Nov. 1929.[41]

With the stock market crash the **critical crisis of 1929-1933** began. It is significant that banks—especially the Morgan bank which was built in conjunction with the primary industries of the two preceding periods (railroads and steel) tried to limit the debacle by artificially supporting the stock prices for United States Steel. But as in previous critical crises, what began as a crisis of the established economic sectors soon became a crisis revealing the breadth of development of the financial branch of capital.

> The depression deepened despite efforts to ease [the] money market and extend credits.... [B]y March 1933... the **banking crisis** deepened and bank holidays blanketed the nation. Industrial output almost halved, unemployment mounted to about 15 million, one third of the nation's railroad mileage was thrown into bankruptcy, and farm mortgage foreclosures were widespread.[42]

Thus began the transition to the dominance of the financiers in the partnership between industrial capital and bank capital. The other major capitalist countries were of course going through the same changes. The worldwide scope of the 1930s depression initiated intense competition among them for a redivision of the world's markets. The outcome of **World War II** established the financiers in the United States as predominant internationally, and this has been reflected politically in the adoption by the U.S. government of the role of "world's policeman." The domestic economic corollary of this has been the **militarization of the economy**. This trend was foreshadowed in the period between world wars when "to the former three basic varieties of commodities—means of production, articles of consumption and articles of luxury—a fourth was now added, occupying an ever more predominant place: instruments of destruction and extermination."[43]

Besides maintaining a standing army in Europe and a worldwide nuclear strike force, since World War II U.S. troops have been used in major wars and interventions in Asia, the Mideast, and the Caribbean (Appendix C). The focus of **foreign policy** in this period has been three-fold. One objective has been to undermine socialism in China and the Soviet Union—the world's largest potential markets for capitalist investment. Another has been to control the world supply and price of oil and thus the competitive potential of European and Japanese manufactured products. A third has been the destruction of socialist revolutions in neocolonies.

Even in this period—despite Keynesian economics—it has been impossible to eliminate intermediate crises, of which there have been seven since the Great Depression (Appendix A). What is most significant about these crises is that every one has been international in scope, that "every international crisis period opens with big monetary upheavals," and that "monetary crises accompany the development of [each] world crisis throughout its duration."[44] The history of the world economy since World War II has been a history of the attempt to finance an international division of labor and to control the **monetary crises** of capitalism. Central to this effort has been the establishment of the International Monetary Fund and the World Bank for financing world development projects.

In the numerous crises of the 1970s we have seen the rise of petrodollars, double-digit inflation, wage and price controls, the devaluation of the dollar, deregulation of the price of gold, record high interest rates, urban bankruptcies, movements against tax increases and deficit spending, and nations on the brink of financial default. Along with the money crises we have also started to see the shift of capital away from "dinosaur" industries in the United States (i.e., industries in deepest crisis like steel and auto) and into the rising stars of the high technology sector. Every trend suggests that the crisis beginning in 1980 is another **critical crisis** posing the historical problem of political-economic realignment.

The South in the Multi-National Economy

What, then, is the role of the national economy of the South in the multi-national economy of the United States? The South is an **economic reserve** area for Northern finance capital. We have seen how the key industries of a capitalist economy change from one period to another. We have also seen that within each period crises reveal the limits of every economic alignment. As these crises intensify and as the **rate of profit** falls in aging industries, capital looks southward to its reserve—the Southern national market with its cheaper labor—for relief.

Relief comes in one main way: through an **industrial shift**. Late in an economic period the industries which are in crisis begin to be transplanted to the South as the North modernizes its economic base. This is how the multi-national system works for the economic benefit of finance capital. Rather than abandoning less profitable industries altogether, their profitability can be stretched out by shifting them southward to take advantage of the cheaper national labor market. At the same time new, more technically advanced industries can be built up in the North, thus revitalizing the production base there. Every shift of old industries to the South results in less demand for skilled labor there than in the technically advancing North. This further reinforces the labor market and national differences between the North and the South.

Even in the era of separate national development before the

Civil War, there was a tendency for the more uniformly agrarian South to pick up the discarded economic activities of the North. A geographical shift in the economics of slave procurement began late in the Experimental Party System period, and a major shift in the old water-powered textile industry occurred late in the Democratizing System period. These shifts foretold the industrial and therefore military ascendance of the North going into the Civil War. In each economic period since that war other industries which developed in the North have been shifted to the South. These shifts involved pig iron production and railroad construction in the late Civil War period; power-loom textiles and lumber in the late Industrial period; and apparel, chemical and defense industries in the late New Deal period.

The first major economic transfer occurred during the period of the Experimental Party System. In the late 1790s, one important focus of merchant activities was the **slave trade**. By 1790 the number of persons sold into slavery in the United States totaled almost seven hundred thousand. The power behind this trade was Northern capital.

> For the northern colonies the West Indian trade was highly profitable. To these islands they sent their surplus grain, fish, staves, horses, and lumber, and in exchange obtained sugar, molasses, and rum, which were sold in home ports at considerable profit. Molasses was especially in demand for it was used in the manufacture of rum. This beverage was the most important item in the highly lucrative slave trade which developed after 1715. Rum was shipped from Newport, Salem, Boston, and New York to the west coast of Africa. Here Negroes were obtained and shipped across the Atlantic to the West Indies, the notorious Middle Passage being used for the purpose. Poor food, unsanitary conditions, and crowded quarters combined to produce an exceptionally high mortality rate during the voyage. Yet, despite this toll, substantial returns accrued. With net profits running 33 per cent or more, the slave trade developed so rapidly that by

1771 there were from sixty to seventy vessels engaged in it, each ship delivering about sixty-five Negroes.[45]

With the invention of the cotton gin in 1793, the possibilities for expanding cotton production resulted in a demand for more slave labor. Thus, after the 1790s the number of slaves in the South rose dramatically (to nearly 4 million at the outbreak of the Civil War). One of the compromises struck between pro- and anti-slavery forces at the Constitutional Convention in 1787 was that the slave trade could not be tampered with for twenty years. Thereafter Congress could legislate against it. This is clearly stated in Article I, Section 9 of the Constitution. In 1808 an Act of Congress finally did ban the slave trade carried on by the Northern merchants. As a result, the border states of the South developed a new enterprise just as heinous in a reverse sort of way as Hitler's death camps in the 1930s and 1940s. These new Southern enterprises were **slave-breeding plantations**, business operations which picked up where the slave trade left off.

During the period of the Democratizing Party System which followed, the development of Southern textiles lagged far behind the **textile industry** in the North. In 1790 when the first cotton was spun by Arkwright machines in Pawtucket, Rhode Island, the source of power was falling water (thus giving rise to the term textile "mill"). By 1830 the mills at Lowell, Massachusetts had begun to employ the belt method of transmitting power to more and more machines. Finally:

> [The] installation of steam power operation in textile mills at Salem and New Bedford (1847) freed the industry from the limitations of water power.[46]

Textiles became the leading industry in the North in the Democratizing period and continued in importance in the Civil War period. When the Northern mills were converting to steam power, the first textile mills in the South were being built up on the old technical basis of water power. This necessitated their concen-

86 THE SOUTH AS AN ECONOMIC RESERVE

tration along the water "fall line" in the lower regions of the Appalachian Mountains (i.e., in the Piedmont, which literally means "at the foot of the mountains"). The cost of using inefficient water power was more than offset by the lower wages in the Southern labor market. Even so, in 1880—near the end of the Civil War Party System—the South had only 5.5 percent of the country's textile spindles (Appendix D).

Other main industries in the United States were **railroads** and **steel**, with steel going mainly into rails and textile machinery. As open hearth steel technology and fabricated metal techniques were introduced in the Northern mills, Southern mills took over more and more crude iron production. Thus by 1890:

> [T]he northern Alabama and adjacent Tennessee district (center: **Birmingham**), with resources of coal as well as iron ore, spurted to 2nd place in pig iron production.[47]

A key related focus of capital in the period of the Civil War Party System was railroads. Here too the South lagged in development until late in the century, when the power and importance of railroad capital began to flag. After the Civil War, capital constructed rail lines at a furious pace between virtually every town in the North. Although the South desperately needed an infrastructure in order to rebuild, the Southern railroad system remained in a shocking state of decay. Those lines which remained open in the South were also a different gauge than those in the North. This necessitated the shifting of cargo from one piece of rolling stock to another at the Baltimore and Cincinnati railheads.

The crisis of railroad capital in the 1870s depression started a shift in railroad investment.

> For all the bond issues and shady railroad politics of the seventies, the Southern states east of the Mississippi had but 13,259 miles of rails by 1880 as compared with 10,609 miles in 1870, an increase of 2,650 miles or only 24.9 per cent. In the decade that followed 14,396 miles were added, making

a total of 27,655 miles, or a gain of 108.6 per cent. Even more rapid was expansion west of the Mississippi, in Texas, Arkansas, and Louisiana, where the increase in mileage during the eighties amounted to 211.4 per cent. In the South as a whole railroads increased from 16,605 miles in 1880 to 39,108 in 1890, or 135.5 per cent as compared with the national expansion of 86.5 per cent.

The construction boom got under way in 1879, during which twice as many miles of rails were laid as in any year since 1873. In the two years following July, 1879, more than $150,000,000 was invested by Northern and foreign capitalists in Southern railroads exclusive of the trans-Mississippi states, and the speculative boom had scarcely begun. Between 1881 and 1890 some 180 new railroad companies, most of them small, opened operations in the South east of the Mississippi. . . .

Simultaneous with the construction boom went a wave of consolidation in which scores of smaller companies were swallowed up by stronger ones. . . .

Other consolidations effected by 1890 placed more than half the railroad mileage of the South in the hands of a dozen large companies and their affiliates. They were very largely directed from New York. . . . The great era of consolidation under Morgan and the New York bankers was not to come until the depression of the nineties.[48]

The other major development in the Southern railroad system late in the period was the adoption of a different gauge track.

Of the numerous disparities that set Southern apart from Northern society, one was entirely man-made: a difference of three inches between the predominant railroad gauges of the two sections. The resultant bottleneck at the Ohio and Potomac border was an awkward and expensive hindrance to traffic. . . . As in other cases of difference, it was the Northern gauge that was regarded as "standard," and the

Southern gauge that had to be "adjusted." After prolonged preparations the day set for changing some 13,000 miles of rails arrived, and traffic was suspended. At dawn on Sunday, May 30, 1886, the Louisville and Nashville, one of the biggest lines involved, had an army of 8,000 men poised along its 2,000 miles of rails, armed with sledge hammers and crowbars and fired with zeal. By sundown their heroic labors had shifted the west rail three inches east along the whole 2,000 miles and adjusted the iron wheels of 300 locomotives and 10,000 pieces of rolling stock to conform to the "standard."[49]

By the beginning of the twentieth century the South had grown strong in several industrial areas which the North originally dominated and then relinquished as unprofitable. These industries, especially pig iron production and mill-powered textiles supported by a relatively new rail system, came to typify the economic mix in the South during the period of the Industrial Party System. But the economic division of labor in the United States did not stand still in this period either.

A shift in **power-loom textiles** occurred during the Industrial Party System period as second-hand machinery was moved south. By the end of that period, the South had well over half of the country's spindles and consumed more than three-quarters of the country's cotton (due to longer hours of work and greater capacity utilization). The advantage in producing textiles in the South is clearly shown in Appendix E: textile wages in the 1920s never exceeded 70 percent of the wages paid for the same work in the North. Since 1930 the number of active spindles in the South has dropped a bit, but the number in the North has declined so precipitously that the Northern nation now accounts for only 1 percent of all spindles (Appendix D).

Another major industry whose center shifted southward in the Industrial Party System period was the **lumber and sawmill industry**. At the beginning of the Industrial period the Northeast and Great Lakes states together produced over half of all lumber products while the South accounted for only 20 percent. At the turn of the century lumber was the fourth most important industry in terms of value added in manufacturing (Figure 4). Finally after 1904—because of the increasing use of other building materials—the lumber industry declined in relative importance in the overall economy. But it continued to grow in the South. By late in the Industrial Party System period the South produced nearly half the country's lumber products (Appendix F).

Just as the Northern economy today is not the same as in the old Industrial period, neither is the Southern economy the same. In all sections of the South the chemicals industry now ranks first or second in importance. Other industries of modern importance are electrical and transportation equipment, machinery, apparel, and food. Their development in the South has been especially intense since the middle of the New Deal Party System period, i.e., since World War II.

The depression of the 1930s hit hard all around the United States but especially devastated those industries whose lives had been prolonged by shifting them south. When Franklin D. Roosevelt took office in 1933, he wasted no time in pronouncing the South "the Nation's No. 1 economic problem."[50] This touched off nearly two decades of highly organized studies of the human and material resources of the South and the prospects for their development. Among these studies were Rupert B. Vance's **Human Geography of the South** (1932), Howard W. Odum's **Southern Regions of the United States** (1936), John V. Van Sickle's **Planning for the South** (1943), and Hoover and Ratchford's **Economic Resources and Policies of the South** (1951).

The last book was written far enough into the New Deal period to show and confirm the pattern of development of Southern industries on the heels of industries previously developed in the North. The **apparel industry** is a good example. In the late 1940s production was—with a few exceptions—still concentrated in the North (Appendix G).

The South's production is concentrated principally in the field of men's clothing, such as dress shirts, pajamas, work shirts and pants, overalls, wash suits, industrial garments, etc. In general these are the cheapest and simplest garments to manufacture. In the products named above, as a whole, the South has approximately a third of the nation's production. The region has very little production in the fields of women's apparel or men's woolen clothing.[51]

Much has changed in the apparel industry since then. In 1950 the South had only 17 percent of the country's apparel workers, well behind the 62 percent in the Northeast. Then the southward shift in the needle trades began in earnest as the profitability of the industry declined in the North. By 1974 it was the South which had the bulk of apparel employment (Appendix G). Mainly, this reflected the decline of New York as the center of the apparel industry. In the South this industry has been organized in a very decentralized pattern. Thus, it is the third largest industry in the South Atlantic states as a whole but doesn't show up in the top three rankings of any state in that area.

The **machinery** and **transportation equipment industries** developed rapidly in the North prior to World War II, but only in the post-war period did these industries start to shift south to any significant degree.

In machinery, the South is making progress both absolutely and relatively. Several textile equipment companies are now producing in the South and at least three of the agricultural machinery companies have located large plants in the region. Between 1939 and 1947, southern employment in the machinery industries increased from 21,000 to about 56,000, thus increasing the relative importance of these industries both in the southern economy and in the industries nationally.[52]

Since the above was written, even more production has been shifted south. Included in this motion are major portions of Allis-

Chalmers' agricultural machinery and General Motors' steering gear operations. At least five new auto plants have been built in the South in response to the industry crisis in the North.[53]

The **food processing industry**, long one of the major sectors of the country's economy, also witnessed its greatest growth in the South in the post-war period.

> Since 1929 this group has had a fairly steady growth, both in absolute size and in relation to national totals. In 1929, the group had 105,000 workers, or 14 per cent of the national total, and produced goods worth about $1-1/4 billion, or 10 per cent of the total for the country. By 1939, the number of workers had increased by 20 per cent and value of products was up by 15 per cent, while outside the South workers were up by 8 per cent and value of product was lower by 15 per cent. From 1939 to 1947, workers in the group in the South increased by 60 per cent, giving the region 18.4 per cent of the national employment, while in the non-South there was an increase of 32.5 per cent. The increase in value added in the South was 216 per cent compared with 150 per cent elsewhere.[54]

This food and agribusiness sector eventually became an important economic base in the political rise of the peanut farmer from Georgia, Jimmy Carter.

In Kirkpatrick Sale's book **Power Shift**, about the "rise of the Southern Rim and its challenge to the eastern establishment,"[55] food, oil, defense, and technology are identified as the four main industrial pillars of the Southern economy today. Surprisingly, Sale completely misses the largest and most important industry in the South today: **chemicals**. In 1975 it was the most important industry in the South Central states and the second most important in the South Atlantic states (Appendix H). In terms of value added in 1980, chemicals ranked first in Virginia, Tennessee, Louisiana, and Texas; second in South Carolina; and third in North Carolina and Alabama.

92 THE SOUTH AS AN ECONOMIC RESERVE

Outside the South the chemical industry is most heavily concentrated in the state of New Jersey, and dominates the combined economies of the Mid-Atlantic states. This industry got its start in the North as a result of World War I, when trade was broken off with Germany—then the world's major supplier of chemicals.

The chemical industry made its greatest gains in the South in the latter part of the New Deal period.

In production workers, the South had approximately 26 per cent of the national total in the chemical group in 1947. On this point the region made no relative gain between 1939 and 1947—in fact, it lost ground slightly. But in value added it increased its share from 16.6 per cent to 20.2 per cent, indicating a considerable increase in productivity per worker. The region got 32 per cent of the expenditures for new plant and equipment made by the group in the nation. It is evident that the industry is preparing for a considerable expansion of its production and as increased emphasis is given to synthetics, plastics, and atomic energy, those preparations would seem to be justified. The South is in a good position to benefit from the expected growth of this industry.[56]

That was the situation and the prospectus in the early 1950s, and the trends perceived then have certainly been more than borne out today.

Another important industry in the New Deal period was oil. Although the **oil industry** had its origins in the 1870s, it received its first big boost when the automobile began to be mass produced. The oil industry developed most rapidly to fuel the war machine in World War II. The war resulted in a vastly expanded system of refining facilities, and oil was readily adopted as a main source of industrial energy. President Eisenhower, the Supreme Allied Commander in that war, was the key figure in politically promoting the economic fortunes of the oil industry.

Dwight Eisenhower was groomed by General Marshall for leadership. He was promoted over 356 more senior officers and was made Allied Commander. Thereafter he was supported by Nelson Rockefeller and his network in order to seize the executive branch for the (Council on Foreign Relations) grouping.... Nationally he increased spending for interstate highways so essential to the expansion of the automobile and petroleum economy.

In the Middle East, Eisenhower secured Iran for the major oil producers through the overthrow of Mossadegh. He established [U.S.] hegemony over Mid-East oil by forcing England and France to back down from their Suez occupation. Under the Eisenhower administration the policy of indirect subsidies to oil producing regimes was instituted, bypassing the Israel lobby.[57]

In the production of crude oil—which is a mining industry, not a manufacturing industry—the South led the nation in 1947. But in terms of value added in refining—which is a manufacturing industry—the North led the way. Indeed, as noted in 1951:

> Over the past two decades, the South's share in this industry has not changed appreciably, although it has had a large absolute growth. In contrast with the conditions prevailing in most other industries, there were indications that in the postwar years the South was losing ground. The region received only about 26 per cent of the expenditures for new plant and equipment made in the industry in 1947.[58]

After 1948, capital investment in other industries rapidly outstripped the oil industry. This was due largely to the shift of refining activities overseas as foreign crude oil was brought into production. At first this forestalled any significant shift of domestic refining to the South. Even in 1975, the only Southern state in which petroleum garnered even a third place rank was Louisiana. Only after the "oil shocks" of the late 1970s has refining been boosted in the South. In 1980 the petroleum industry ranked first in Mississippi, second in Louisiana and Texas, and third in Oklahoma. But it also ranks among the top three industries in five western states as well.[59]

Two other major industries which made their main appearance in the New Deal period are **defense** and **electronics**. They are related because the Pentagon has funded most of the research and development in modern electronics since World War II. Two sections of the electronics industry must be distinguished. One section is the older **electrical equipment industry** which produces commodities based on tubes and passive components such as resistors and capacitors. This part of the industry is not nearly as technically sophisticated as the semiconductor electronics sector based on integrated circuits and micro-computers. The former employs a high proportion of unskilled and semi-skilled labor whereas the latter often employs more engineers and technicians than production workers. The older electrical section of the industry has been transplanted into states like Virginia, Tennessee, and Arkansas.

There has been a steady flow of [electrical equipment] firms out of New York (its birth place) for more than three decades, and many of these firms have moved South. Late last year [1976] Stackpole Carbon, a components producer, pulled up its stakes in Kane, Pennsylvania, and headed for Lincolnton, North Carolina. "It's a matter of economics," according to the head of Stackpole, "Pennsylvania is a high labor area. It was felt that we had to get out of the resistor business or relocate." Litton Industries has established plants in Columbia, South Carolina and Goldsboro, North Carolina. Ampex moved its assembly of consumer tape cassettes to Opelika, Alabama in 1973. Magnavox started TV assembly production in Tennessee in 1973, and GTE Sylvania recently moved its color TV assembly operations from Batavia, New York to Smithfield, North Carolina. In all, more than 330 electronics manufacturing plants were operating in the Southeastern states in 1976.[60]

The newer **electronics** section remains based in California and Massachusetts. It produces computers and other high technology office and industrial equipment and supplies military-space electronics for aircraft and missiles. This defense-oriented **aerospace industry** began to move South in the 1960s.

Except for a few World War Two era aircraft plants (for example Lockheed's Marietta, Georgia factory), these industries are all fundamentally new to the region, and most are grouped around the various National Aeronautics and Space Administration (NASA) facilities which ring the South. Thus in the Cape Kennedy area of Florida there are now a host of aerospace and electronics firms in the growing Orlando-Titusville-Melbourne industrial triangle. Half of Alabama's top twenty military-space contractors are grouped around NASA's Marshall Space Flight Center in Huntsville, and almost all of these are engaged in the development of missiles and electronic warfare systems. In Texas, the location of NASA's Manned Space Center in Houston gave impetus to the growth of electronics companies like Texas Instruments... in the Dallas-Fort Worth area. With the increasing use of electronic sub-systems in fighter plane construction, major military aircraft manufacturers also expanded operations there. Only in North Carolina was the pattern somewhat different: there AT&T's Western Electric Division became a major aerospace and electronics contractor for the military on the basis of its well-established electrical equipment manufacturing and research operations in the three Piedmont cities of Burlington, Greensboro, and Winston-Salem....

It is also an outstanding feature of these highly technical military-oriented industries that scientific and other non-production line personnel comprise up to 60 percent of all employees, whereas semi- and unskilled workers account for as little as 16 percent of employment. Consequently, unlike apparel firms dependent on unskilled manual labor, these in-

96 THE SOUTH AS AN ECONOMIC RESERVE

dustries have not needed to seek locations in the South with an expanding supply of wage labor, i.e., in [its traditional core area]. Instead, the aerospace/electronics complexes in the region have been situated [on the periphery of this core], thus . . . gradually supplanting the once principal division of labor . . . between textile centers and the plantation belt, with a regional division of labor between industries employing mostly mental and technical or mostly manual and unskilled labor.[61] [see Map, p. 98]

This trend in aerospace production underlies the heavy shift of defense contracting to the South from 1965 to 1970 (Appendix I).

Since the early 1970s the industrial economy of the Northern nation has been sliding into a prolonged crisis reminiscent of critical crises of the past. Correspondingly, the basic industries of the New Deal Party System period are being shifted to the South. The arms industry which grew out of World War II is no exception. It was one of Roosevelt's own hand-picked New Deal statesmen—Lyndon Baines Johnson—who began to effect the transfer of defense and aerospace industries to the South.

The **computer industry** is the hottest new industry in the world and one which the United States virtually controls. Contrary to Sale's projection in **Power Shift**, this industry has **not** begun to shift South because it is a rising industry and is not in crisis.

Which regions produced the ten states where population grew most in the 1970's? Ask a well-informed group of friends that question and it is a good bet that many will correctly answer that none of the boom states was in the Northeast or Midwest.

Most likely, they will confidently predict that about half, maybe more, of the fastest-growing states were in the South. Not so.

Only one of these states, Florida, is in the South. The remaining nine are in the West. . . .

More and more, the sunrise industries of the new information age are opening up facilities in the Rocky Mountain states of the Old West....

The present North-South shift is really a spreading out, a thinning out of [high technology] industry from the overpopulated Northeast to the wide-open space of the Southwest and West.[62]

High technology industries (including robotics, genetic engineering, etc.) represent capital's hopes for the reindustrialization of the North and West and for entering a new political-economic period.

Even if the economy were eventually reorganized on a high-technology basis, history confirms that the new period would bring more intermediate crises, a steady shift of mature industries southward, and ultimately another critical crisis. For workers in the North this can only mean more periods of **job dislocations and unemployment**; for workers in the South it means continued **exploitation** of their labor for wages that are much lower than in the North.

These conditions have confronted workers in other periods of economic transition. Why has the working class in this country— especially the huge working class in the Northern nation— historically put up with these conditions? How has capital been able to politically pre-empt the development of **revolutionary movements** in the North in every one of these crises? How are workers drawn into a new political alignment and a new economic period of boom and bust? Given that politics is the concentrated expression of economics, it is not surprising to find that the answer again lies in the South. The South is not only an economic reserve for capital but also a reserve of political strength.

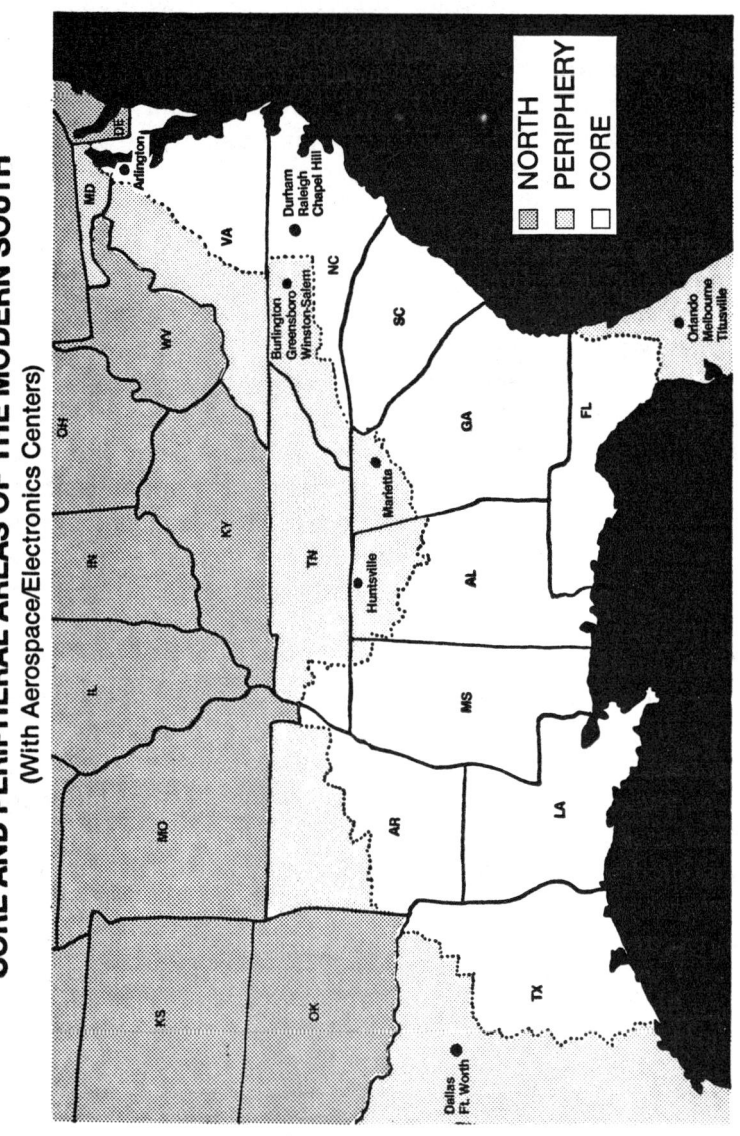

CORE AND PERIPHERAL AREAS OF THE MODERN SOUTH
(With Aerospace/Electronics Centers)

Adapted from: Allen, **The Negro Question in the United States**; Keller, "The Militarization of the Southern Economy," 41-44.

4.

The South as a Political Reserve

A few years ago I had an interview for a teaching job in the South. This interview and subsequent events reveal something about the attitudes of Northerners and Southerners toward each other. During the interview we talked about my qualifications for the job, what the employer was looking for, and the work itself. At the end of this interview I was asked a question I had never before had to field: "How would you feel about living in the South?" The interviewers were clearly concerned about whether a Northerner could accept and adjust to the real differences between North and South. I replied that while I had no illusions about the fact that the North and South are indeed different I also had no apprehensions that would prevent me from moving to the South.

Later I told a colleague at a major Midwestern university about the interview. He was in a position to interview applicants from around the country for similar work in the North. I asked him if he asked Southerners whether they had any apprehensions about moving to the North. Without a moment's hesitation he replied, "No, because we wouldn't consider them in the first place!"

This anecdote reflects the political attitudes of Northerners and Southerners toward each other. Since the Civil War, people in the Northern nation have thought of the colonized Southern nation as inferior, and this has been expressed in rampant Northern **chauvinism**. In turn, Southerners—white and black—realize that they have been relegated to an inferior position. Southerners justifiably resent being looked down upon and being treated as second-class citizens by Northerners.

One inevitable result has been the disruption of **labor unity** between Northern and Southern workers in their common confrontations with capital in the economic and political arenas. Historically, the Northern worker has been persuaded that the inferior status of the South works to his personal advantage. Only when capital has found it necessary to implement **social reforms** in the South to conform to the labor requirements for a new industrial shift to the South has the Northern labor movement been urged to interact with the South. The rationale for such mobilization is usually stated in terms of **morality**, i.e., to "better" the South. But the result of those actions (by Abolitionists, Carpetbaggers, Freedom Riders, etc.) has never been the elimination of the **colonized status** of the Southern nation. And so long as the South functions as an economic reserve for Northern capital, it will also function as a **political reserve** and source of strength for capital.

This political strength is of immense importance in controlling the political development of the huge labor movement in the North. Although every critical crisis has brought an upsurge in the economic and political activity of workers, in no instance has the working class successfully developed a political program based on its **class interests**. The historical evidence of this is that the **labor vote** has remained tied to either the Democratic or Republican party. It is the economic and political control of the colonized South which has always dictated this outcome.

Capital, Labor, and Revolutionary Crises

Every period in the development of the economy is marked at its beginning and end by **critical crises**. In each critical crisis the sections of the capitalist class with investments in old industries and those tied to rising industries come into conflict over how to further develop the economy. The representatives of the old section of the economy favor economic programs that would save their capital investments from the effects of the crisis. Newer industries which haven't reached the limits of their expansion require a different economic program. Their interest is to promote the growth of the industries of the future rather than to protect and prolong the life of less profitable, old industrial sectors.

The **political split** between opposing sectors of capital can be seen in current policy debates about how to resolve the economic depression of the 1980s.

The natural tendency of capital is to flow into the most advanced means of production, a tendency that also exacerbates the tendency to overproduce. But the financier has little choice when it comes to a decision to subsidize unproductive industries **or** to invest in the most productive means of production.

The global shift of capital away from energy and to production of the hardware and software of the new technology, and its integration into production and circulation, is already in progress. It is the financier's dream to fully exploit this process. Their vision is one of the export of advanced technology from the industrialized nations to the newly industrialized neocolonies who would in turn export cheap commodities to the advanced industrial countries.

The attempt to implement this vision will not go unopposed. Powerful old sectors of the US economy such as auto, steel, rubber, shipbuilding, airframe, and textiles are hungry for investment and protection. These sectors are ready to fight for policies that will funnel investment into other coffers. The struggle between these general camps of the bourgeoisie for control of social revenues and access to investment capital underlie much of the bitter struggle around policy within the US ruling class.[1]

That policy struggle is boiling down to a fight between the proponents of **reindustrialization** and **supply-side economics**.

The economic policy debate is being posed as a struggle between the advocates of "industrial policy" or "reindustrialization," in which government would play an active role in fostering certain sectors of the economy; and advocates of a "hands-off" or "supply-side" type of approach. The basic question being fought out is which bourgeois grouping will control government intervention in favor of investments benefitting its sector of the economy.

The spokesmen for the older industrial sectors and the traditional military suppliers fight for increased fiscal stimulus, easy money protection for steel, tax breaks and subsidies for housing construction and other industries, dismantling controls on pollution and programs aimed at subsidizing the unemployed and poor, and, of course, increased military spending.

Opposed to this sector is the modern financier who needs to facilitate capital flow into the growing areas of the economy and who is, now, less able to afford the price of concessions to less productive, older sectors. In the realm of policy, these descendants of the CFR [Council on Foreign Relations]-Trilateral-free traders are proposing a spectrum of "industrial policy" alternatives.[2]

What is happening today in the political arena is typical of every critical crisis. A political split develops within the capitalist class, and a certain period of indecision prevails. For the capitalist class this represents not only an economic and political crisis within its own ranks but also a potential **revolutionary crisis** with regard to the working class.

A shifting of political balance must necessarily ensue, as with every other shift in the control of the decisive form of wealth. The struggle between the newcomers and the grouping that controlled political power on the basis of a previously decisive form of wealth is bound to bring about a destabilization and, as with every struggle within the ruling class, it is bound to create the conditions for a revolutionary upsurge on the part of the workers.[3]

A split within the capitalist class is, therefore, one **primary condition for social revolution**. A **second condition** is the impossibility of continuing to live and work on the basis of outmoded forms of production which have fallen into crisis. The working class sees this condition expressed most clearly in rising levels of **unemployment** and **poverty**. Within the organized labor movement the impact is especially intense for unions and their membership. More than a century ago it was observed that in periods of economic expansion the natural tendency for capital to concentrate labor in factories lays the basis for the **rise of labor organizations**.

> But with the development of industry the proletariat not only increases in number; it becomes concentrated in greater masses, its strength grows, and it feels that strength more.... The growing competition among the bourgeois, and the resulting commercial crises, make the wages of the workers ever more fluctuating. The unceasing improvement of machinery, ever more rapidly developing, makes their livelihood more and more precarious; the collisions between individual workmen and individual bourgeois take more and more the character of collisions between two classes. Thereupon the workers begin to form combinations (Trades' Unions) against the bourgeois; they club together in order to keep up the rate of wages; they found permanent associations to make provision beforehand for these occasional revolts. Here and there the contest breaks out into riots.[4]

Conversely, the breakdown of production disperses workers and provides the impetus for the **decline of labor organizations** designed to protect and defend their interests. With these organizations in disarray, and ineffective as a result of a critical crisis, life in the old way becomes impossible for labor.

The history of the trade union movement in the United States reflects the historical sequence of critical crises and political-economic realignments. The first trade unions were called **city**

trade unions. They covered a particular trade within a particular city and arose at the start of the Experimental Party System period in 1794. Many were weak and disintegrated in the intermediate crisis of 1796-1798. The city trade unions were reorganized during the business upswing beginning in 1806, only to disintegrate again in the critical crisis of 1815-1821. City trade unions were the highest form of labor organization in the Experimental period.

Along with new industries come new organizations of the working class. The Democratizing Party System period witnessed the rise of **city trade centrals** (CTCs). These were city-wide federations of different trades—similar to Central Labor Councils today. The first CTCs appeared in Philadelphia in 1827. Their number had increased to thirteen by 1836. In 1834 these CTCs joined to form the first national labor organization, the National Trades Federation, with a central office to coordinate their activities. The CTCs and the National Trades Federation disintegrated in the intermediate crisis of 1837-1843.

Beginning in 1852 the different trades started to reorganize as separate **national trade unions** (NTUs) without any central office uniting them. Many of these NTUs disintegrated in the critical crisis of 1857-1858.

In the period of the Civil War Party System, the movement to form NTUs was revived as a result of the war-induced increase in industrial production and the whittling away of real wages by inflation. By 1873 there were twenty-six different national trade unions with a total of three hundred thousand members. The intermediate crisis of 1873-1877 totally devastated these organizations, and their number dropped to only nine functioning unions covering fifty thousand members.

Between 1866 and 1872 the newly formed National Labor Union grew in numbers and influence. In 1872 it was transformed into the National Labor Reform Party and subsequently died in the 1873-1877 crisis.

In 1878 the first **industrial union** (i.e., not based in any particular trade) in the United States was organized in the North. It was called the Knights of Labor, and by 1886 it had almost six thousand branches or assemblies covering seven hundred thousand members. In 1882 the American Federation of Labor (AFL) was formed on a trades basis and began to grow at the expense of the Knights of Labor. In the early 1890s the AFL had surpassed the Knights of Labor in terms of membership, and the latter disintegrated and disappeared during the critical crisis of 1893-1897.

The AFL became the first major labor organization to survive a critical crisis (1893-1897), although its growth came to a grinding halt during the 1890s.

During the new Industrial Party System period there was a significant attempt at labor organization along industrial lines by the Industrial Workers of the World (IWW). Formed in 1905, the IWW was a **revolutionary union** in the sense that it wanted workers to control the production process and receive the profits as well as the wages earned by their labor. But it had no political program for achieving these objectives. The IWW dissolved during the intermediate crisis of 1920-1921 after reaching a peak membership of over one hundred thousand during World War I.

The AFL continued to organize skilled tradesmen on the basis of **business unionism** (as opposed to the IWW's revolutionary approach). During the prosperous times after the turn-of-the-century the AFL grew rapidly to over 1.5 million members. It experienced small losses of membership during the intermediate crises of 1903-1904, 1907-1908, and 1913-1914. Then war production and inflation ballooned the AFL ranks to over 4 million members in 1920. The intermediate crisis of 1920-1921 cut membership by one-third. During the subsequent boom period many former AFL members were organized into **company-run unions**, as was also the tendency in fascist Italy and Germany. The critical crisis of 1929-1933 demolished AFL hopes for a resurgence and dropped its membership to half its 1920 level. Company unions continued to expand at the expense of the AFL.

The Great Depression gave rise to another major labor organization—the Congress of Industrial Organizations (CIO)— which split from the AFL in 1938 and organized 5 million industrial workers by 1943 (compared to fewer than 4 million in the AFL). Except during the intermediate crisis of 1948-1949, both the AFL and the CIO continued to grow during and after World War II. In 1955 the two organizations merged to form the AFL-CIO, with a joint membership of 16 million. During the subsequent crises of 1957-1958 and 1960-1961 the AFL-CIO lost 1.5 million members. Then it lost the United Auto Workers Union as an affiliate following the 1966-1967 crisis. AFL-CIO membership reached nearly 17 million by 1974 before declining as a result of the crisis of the mid-1970s. After 1976, membership rolls again rose to over 17 million.

The critical crisis which began in the early 1980s caused AFL-CIO membership to drop significantly, and current estimates place it at only 13.7 million. Due to the current crisis, the percentage decline in membership in specific unions has been 42 percent among steelworkers, 39 percent for machinists, 31 percent for rubberworkers, 27 percent for autoworkers, 22 percent for teamsters, and 17 percent among garment workers.[5]

As the post-war series of crises built toward the current critical crisis, the labor movement began to suffer. Based in the declining industries of the North, the organized labor movement now encompasses only 20 percent of the workforce in the United States. The labor movement clearly cannot continue in the same old way if it is to survive. It faces a **revolutionary crisis**.

Two examples of organized labor's **defensive reaction** to the crisis of the 1980s come from the United Auto Workers. The auto industry is part of the old complex of industries which characterizes the economic period just ending. With as many as three hundred thousand autoworkers laid off since the late 1970s, the UAW leadership has been trying desperately to cope with the crisis. It has urged **contract concessions** to the auto companies in order to keep them in business. This was especially true in the case of Chrysler, which the banks refused to save from bankruptcy unless the workers granted major concessions. Ford and GM also obtained concessions, but GM has continued to shift production out of the country and has contracted to import certain makes of cars from Japanese producers. This is all part of the objective motion toward a new **international division of labor**. No amount of UAW concessions will restore the U.S. auto industry to its former heights.

The other defensive action taken by the UAW was its remerger with the AFL-CIO in 1981, in hopes of being able to draw on the greater financial and political resources of the federation in order to lobby for its interests. But this action cannot restore autoworkers to jobs which are no longer profitable to capital.

Labor Revolts and Third Parties

During critical crises and serious intermediate crises labor has always sought ways to express its **class interests** separately from those of capital. Inevitably, the old forms of labor organization are weakened in a crisis, thus making peaceful bargaining a toothless weapon. The crisis within capital also leaves business few resources with which to bargain. In such moments business is likely to demand **concessions** or **givebacks** from workers. For these reasons, during severe crises workers turn more and more to other forms of economic and political action to secure their interests. Their methods of struggle have included strikes, general strikes, rebellions, and the formation of third parties. The method of suppression has been the all-round use of the arms of the **state**, including the army, police, courts and prisons. This reveals that **capital** actually controls the state and uses it in its class interests.

The critical crisis of 1784-1788 brought the U.S. political system to life. It was marked by Shay's Rebellion, a major revolt of debt-ridden farmers in western Massachusetts.

In response to the intermediate crisis of 1796-1798 during the Experimental Party System period, efforts were made to levy a direct federal tax on homeowners in order to raise money for the military. This gave rise to the Fries Uprising in Pennsylvania. The intermediate crisis of 1807-1809 and the critical crisis of 1815-1821 were characterized by so many labor actions that state governments initiated **conspiracy trials** against trade unionists for being "seditious."

Within the Democratizing Party System period there were three instances of intense labor unrest. During the intermediate crisis of 1833-1834, Irish laborers working on the Chesapeake and Ohio canal staged a rebellion which was put down with the first use-ever of federal troops against workers. The crisis of 1837-1843 was an especially heavy strike period and gave rise to the movement for a ten-hour day in the United States. The critical crisis of 1857-1858 led to a **general strike** of more than twenty thousand workers in New England in 1860.

In the period of the Civil War Party System, labor actions during crises became bigger and more militant. During the 1873-1877 depression there were numerous incidents including an 1874 **rebellion** in New York City which was provoked when police charged a labor rally in Tompkins Square. The mid-1870s also saw the high point of activities by the secret miners' organization called the Molly Maguires.

During 1877 there was a major strike among railroad workers. With some troops still occupying four Southern states and other troops without pay due to Congress' failure to pass an appropriations bill, railroad workers took over rail facilities in the North in protest against **wage cuts**. Militia were raised to "recapture" yards from the men who ran them. Troops who were willing to fight without pay were also sent into action. Pitched battles ensued in Baltimore, Pittsburgh, West Virginia, Chicago, and St. Louis, but in the end the workers were defeated. As a result of this strike, **conspiracy laws** were revived in many states.

The crisis of 1882-1885 culminated in the 1886 **general strike** in Chicago and the Haymarket Square Massacre of labor demonstrators by police. The crisis of 1890-1891 resulted in a massive strike by steelworkers at the Carnegie Steel Company in Homestead, Pennsylvania in 1892. After repulsing three hundred Pinkerton detectives hired by the company, the strikers were overcome by state militia, with lives lost on both sides. Two days later **martial law** was declared in the silver mines of Idaho as striking miners repulsed strikebreakers but succumbed to intervening federal troops.

The 1894 Pullman Strike highlighted the critical crisis of 1893-1897. More than three thousand federal marshalls and additional federal troops were used to prevent a takeover of the railroad system like that which occurred during the 1877 strike. Both incidents revealed the significance of railroad capital in the period.

The first crisis of the new Industrial Party System period was marked by the Great Anthracite Coal Strike of 1902. The immediate post-World War I crisis witnessed a major strike among unorganized steelworkers. At the same time, between 1918 and 1920, the IWW was viciously attacked by federal courts and was destroyed by arrests. The Palmer Raids of 1920-1921 (organized by Attorney General A. Mitchell Palmer) resulted in the arrests of three thousand labor organizers in thirty-three cities. Many were put on trial for "criminal syndicalism" (illegal labor organizing) and those who were immigrants suffered **deportation**.

The period came to an end with the critical crisis of 1929-1933. The most militant labor action developed in the old textile industry—especially in North Carolina, Tennessee, and New Jersey. But there was also the Bonus Army March on Washington by impoverished veterans in 1932. It was dispersed with the use of federal infantry, cavalry, and tanks under the command of General Douglas MacArthur, assisted by Major Dwight D. Eisenhower.

During the 1937-1938 crisis in the New Deal Party System period, autoworkers seized General Motors plants in Flint, Michigan. Ultimately this strike involved over one hundred thousand workers. **Sit-down strikes** spread to other industries —including rubber, steel, textiles, petroleum, and shipbuilding —and resulted in a **general strike** by half-a-million workers. The Memorial Day Massacre of striking steelworkers occurred in Chicago in 1937 when police opened fire on union demonstrators outside Republic Steel. Out of this tragedy emerged the organization of steelworkers by the CIO, but further use of sit-down strikes was threatened with federal military response after the Supreme

Court declared such "occupations" illegal.

The post-World War II strike by four hundred thousand bituminous coal miners resulted in President Truman's order for federal troops to take over the mines in 1946. Truman also ordered troops to seize the steel mills in 1952, and the use of federal troops against workers became a more open threat in this period. Backed up by this threat, the use of **injunctions**—as provided for in the Taft-Hartley Act of 1947—became common. When issued against workers threatening to strike, these injunctions have served as clear warnings that federal intervention is imminent. This threat—coupled with the generally expanding economic conditions of the post-war period—has limited the development of significant **class confrontations** since the 1950s.

But there have been some incidents of militant labor action in the present period. Not surprisingly, the main area of struggle has been in the chief industry in which labor's bargaining rights were not officially recognized by the National Labor Relations Act of 1935: agriculture. In the 1960s the farm workers on the West Coast struggled valiantly against violent repression in order to organize under the banner of the United Farm Workers. Since then the Texas Farm Workers Union, the Farm Labor Organizing Committee in the Midwest, and other bodies have carried on the fight for the organization of **farm labor**. Insofar as the farmworkers movement has been officially recognized by the California government and growers, this represents the final stage in the process of integrating the labor movement into the political structure of the New Deal Party System. It marks the end of an era.

Finally, witness the changing attitude of autoworkers to the demand for **concessions** by Chrysler in the early 1980s. In 1979 U.S. Chrysler workers were led by union officials to "renegotiate" their contract with the company and ended up giving back wages and benefits previously acquired. In 1982, when the company started showing a profit, the workers demanded the return of some of their givebacks. When the leadership negotiated a new contract with virtually no gains, the workers voted to reject it—the first time that has happened since World War II—but continued working until a new agreement could be reached. In Canada the Chrysler workers went even further and struck against the company's demands for concessions rather than work without a contract.

This new **labor militancy** is a sign of the times in a country which has seen decades of **labor peace** due to a long period of economic prosperity. With the prolonged crisis of the 1980s the conditions for labor peace are rapidly disintegrating. The old **labor leadership** is likewise proving ineffectual in representing labor's new demands. Those leaders know only how to deal with capital as a "partner in production" and not as the adversary the struggle against concessions showed it to be. Consequently the stage is set for the decline of the old union structures and the reorienting of union activity along more militant lines. This motion is consistent with history and the demands of the current critical crisis.

All of these strikes, general strikes, and rebellions were **spontaneous**; that is, they developed in reaction to unfavorable economic actions taken against workers as a result of crises. In no instance was there a planned, **conscious** effort to disarm the forces which were sent against workers. And just as there was no military strategy, so too there was no political strategy for workers to gain political power and defeat the rule of capital.

Spontaneity is inherently limited in what it can achieve. It can signal capital that labor is extremely discontent with the conditions of its existence and that if capital wishes to continue to exploit labor it will have to **reform** its ways. Indeed, that is the essence of every new program of **labor legislation** implemented by the ruling party in each new political-economic alignment. But labor itself has never gone far enough to establish the conditions for the abolition of crises and the rule of capital.

In each critical crisis and during the major intermediate crises, the political conditions were ripe for the mobilization of workers into a **third party of labor** and for the espousal of political programs reflecting the particular interests of labor. A simple indicator of this is the number of seats held in Congress by Representatives and Senators not affiliated with either of the two main parties in each party system period (Appendix J). At the beginning of every realignment this number increases dramatically, persists for a number of years as the realignment process continues, and then declines as political realignment is completed and economic expansion begins. Intermediate crises tend to revive splits in the political ranks of capital and renew independent political activity among workers. Thus at various critical and intermediate crisis points, third parties appear. Some are led by labor figures and some by dissenting capitalists, but all vie for the **labor vote**.

Some of the most notable third parties which have arisen in U.S. history were the Workingmen's Party (founded in 1828), the Liberty Party (1839), the Free Soil Party (1848), the National Labor Reform Party (1872), the Greenback Party (1876), the Populist Party (1889), the Farmer-Labor Party (1920), the AFL-promoted Labor Party (1936), and the Progressive Party (1948). The post-World War II era is replete with examples of splits in the two main parties and the rise of third parties (the States Rights Party, the American Independent Party, and the Citizens Party).

No third party movement to date has been able to win the vast majority of workers away from the programs and promises of the main parties. Thus, the rule of capital has persisted and the cycle of devastating crises has continued to impact on generation after generation of workers. This is possible because capital has developed a **political reserve** which enables it to make all sorts of grand promises to labor in order to co-opt any independent political activity by workers and keep them in the fold. That resource for thwarting third party movements is the so-called "Solid South."

The Theory of the Southern Strategy

The normal development of the capitalist economic system ends in critical crises. Capitalists split over the question of economic development policy, and these splits condition an upsurge of independent political activity among workers. Workers represent a force with the potential to reorganize society on a non-crisis oriented—i.e., non-capitalist—basis. Their independent activity is therefore a grave threat to the rule of capital. The main source of this threat is the labor movement in the North because of its concentration in big industries and because of its experience with methods of organization. Therefore, during crises a primary objective of capital has been to prevent the independent political development of workers by **co-opting** the labor movement into political parties led by the representatives of capital.

To divert labor from an independent political path, these representatives of capital need some sort of strategy. That strategy is typically called the **Southern strategy**.

The key element in the Southern strategy is the existence of a politically **Solid South** in which Southern labor is tightly controlled. Before the Civil War there could be no free labor movement in the South on a scale like that in the North because the main form of labor was slavery. After the Civil War the Southern nation became a colony of the North, and the development of the labor movement there has been systematically restricted by law ever since.

The weakness of labor in the South has historically given a free hand to the careerism of the most reactionary political leaders in the country. The South is well known for its perennial crop of politicians with fascist, white supremacist, and openly anti-labor views. These men are the open spokesmen of the true views of capital toward working men and women of any color. Because of the **suppression of organized labor in the South**, these politicians are virtually immune from recall and from being voted out of office.

It is no wonder that the politicians with the greatest **congressional seniority** typically come from the South, and that because of that seniority they always sit on and often chair the most powerful committees in Congress. Thus they control much of the major legislation in this country. If it is favorable to capital it will be given their stamp of approval; if it is favorable to labor it can be killed in committee.

This is a main weapon for capital in its continual struggle for advantage over labor.

114 THE SOUTH AS A POLITICAL RESERVE

[T]he South politically controls the country and Wall Street controls the South. The people of New York or California did not vote for Senator Eastland of Mississippi, but his 22 years in the Senate [allowed] him to head the decisive Judiciary Committee. Therefore, he effectively [controlled] legislation for the whole country. This legislative control of the country through the South is a main weapon in bourgeois democracy.[6]

Credit for this formulation has been given to the great black scholar Dr. W.E.B. Du Bois. His explanation of this **political formula** was one of the most important themes in his masterwork **Black Reconstruction in America** (published in 1935). The formulation can be traced back even further to an 1861 statement.

The progressive abuse of the Union by the slave power, working through its alliance with the Northern Democratic Party, is, so to say, the **general formula of United States history** since the beginning of this century.[7] [emphasis added]

What Du Bois achieved was an explanation of how the pre-Civil War alliance between labor in the Northern Democratic Party and capital in the Southern Democratic Party was preserved in the post-Civil War periods.

At first glance this appears to be an impossible alliance. How could such a relationship—i.e., between the huge labor movement in the North and the most vocal critics of labor in the South—ever last? The answer to this question is also the answer to why there has never been a successful **third party of labor**. Strategic positions within the Congress are perennially occupied by reactionary Southern Democrats. On this basis, the reactionaries have the positions and power to come forward with legislative promises, bargains, and compromises which—as happened in the 1930s—offer labor a "New Deal."

The catch is that labor must stay within the political party which can best secure this deal with the Solid South. The argument goes like this: If the Democrats can carry the North and the South goes solidly Democratic, the Democratic Party will win a majority of the seats in the House and Senate and the Southern Democrats will be returned to power in the all-important legislative committees in Congress. Then the Democrats can guarantee passage of legislation favorable to labor. However, what they actually pass is legislation appropriate to the expansion of the economy on a new technological and industrial basis. Insofar as this facilitates a boom period for capitalism, new jobs are created and labor is lulled into a sense of success and security until the system shatters on the rocks of another critical crisis. In the meantime, capital maintains control of the government and can also legislate directly against labor and in its own interests if necessary.

The only alternative for labor is to take an independent political course, build its political strength to the point where it can gain **state power**, and then reorganize the economy on a non-crisis oriented, non-capitalist basis. But the leaders of the Democratic Party say that can't work, and they point to the solid Democratic South as proof. Their argument is this: If Northern labor goes for a third party, this will split the Democratic Party and make it impossible for it to win. This will mean loss of Congressional control and thus the impossibility of delivering any "new deal." The only hope for a third party of labor rests on its ability to defeat the Republican Party. To do this the labor vote has to be united. But the labor vote in the South is so rigidly controlled by the Democratic Party machine there that, in fact, the South would remain Democratic and effectively split the labor vote. Thus in the end the Republicans would always win against a third party of labor.

This scenario is revived every time there is an upsurge in the independent political activity of labor. It is the source of the warnings propagated during elections that "to vote for a third party is to throw away your vote" and that labor has no real choice but to "vote for the lesser of two evils." This **ideology** is simply the capitalists' argument against independent political activity by labor. They can "prove" the correctness of these arguments and reinforce this ideology by actually using the Solid South to thwart the success of any third party at the polls.

President Coolidge made it clear that this political strategy for controlling the Northern labor movement is **consciously** understood by capital. In 1930 he said:

> It does not seem likely that any attempt made in the near future to start another political party could succeed. It is an enormous undertaking that requires the force of some great moral upheaval to make it effective.[8]

The required upheaval is not, however, a moral one. What is required is a critical crisis and a split in the political ranks of capital. Coolidge continued:

> So far as now appears, any new party would have to be radical.[9]

That is certainly true since the real problem for labor is the continued existence of capitalism itself. But:

> [B]ecause the Democratic Party has had the solid South without much regard to issues, it has usually tried to appeal to the radicals of the North.[10]

On this basis workers have always been weaned away from third party activity and have ended up believing:

> that all necessary reforms can be secured within the old parties and that they are the best instruments of government.[11]

Thus labor in the Northern nation has historically been trapped in a seemingly inescapable contradiction. On one hand, capital can use political control of the colonized South to defeat third party movements by labor. On the other hand, labor's only electoral ally is that same Solid South. Du Bois noted this dilemma long ago.

THE THEORY OF THE SOUTHERN STRATEGY 117

The South does and must vote for reaction. There can be, therefore, neither in the South nor in the nation a successful third party movement.... A solid bloc of reaction in the South can always be depended upon to unite with Northern conservatism to elect a president.... [Yet] wherever a liberal and democratic party started to differentiate itself... **the only alliance offered was the broken oligarchy of the South.**[12] [emphasis added]

This contradiction clarifies some political facts of life for the working class in the Northern nation.

So long as the Democratic Party machine in the Southern nation controls the black and white labor vote there, Northern labor cannot expect a third party to gain political power through **electoral politics**. One alternative which the Northern working class will have to come to grips with is the question of insurrection against the state. This is a course other working classes have been forced to take in order to escape the stranglehold of capitalist "democracy," which is contrived, controlled, and not democratic at all.

For there to be any chance for the electoral success of a third party movement, a necessary precondition is the destruction of the Southern Democratic political machine or the elimination of its role and influence in Northern politics. Since the United States is a multi-national country with the Southern nation held in a direct colonial status, an obvious strategy would be the political **separation** of the two nations. Not only would this strengthen the political position of labor in the North, but it would also weaken the grip of Northern capital on the Southern worker. This is a question which workers will have to deal with seriously if an end is to be put to this crisis-oriented system. As one contemporary working class leader has proposed:

> It is obvious that the working class movement in the [Northern] Nation is strangled by the political representatives of Wall Street from the South. There is no way for the [Northern]

workers to vote these fascists out of office, yet these Southern stooges of Wall Street legislate for the whole [United States]. There is but one proper slogan and that is the slogan for a separation of the [Southern] Nation from the [Northern] Nation.

In a parallel situation, Marx wrote:

"Quite apart from all the phrases about 'international' and humane justice for Ireland... it is in the direct and absolute interest of the English working class to get rid of their present connection with Ireland. And this is my fullest conviction, and for reasons which in part I cannot tell the English workers themselves. For a long time, I believed that it would be possible to overthrow the Irish regime by English working class ascendancy. I always expressed this point of view in the **New York Tribune**. Deeper study has now convinced me of the opposite. The English working class will never accomplish anything until it has got rid of Ireland.... English reaction in England has its roots in the subjugation of Ireland."

It is from the concrete realities of our political lives, and from the theoretical understanding of a century of struggle against national oppression that we, in the name of the [Northern] working class demand the independence and freedom of the [Southern] Nation.[13]

The quotation about the English working class and the **Irish question** points out how the colonized status of Ireland was used to block the independent political development of English workers. In the United States the analogous situation is the **Southern question** and the political use of the colonized Southern nation to control the Northern working class.

The Two-Party System Through the Civil War

It would be a mistake to say that only the leaders of the Democratic Party use the Southern strategy to the advantage of the sections of capital they represent. The Republicans also have the ability to work it to their advantage. Obviously, the Republican Party does not control the Southern Democratic machine directly. But history has endowed the Republicans with indirect influence over that wing of the Democrats. For example, only with the support of the Southern Democratic representatives called the **boll weevils** was President Reagan able to pass and implement his "supply-side" economic programs in 1981.

The history of **political party development** in the United States reveals the connections between the different economic classes in society and the **two-party political structure**. It also shows how party tactics for implementing the Southern strategy have taken shape in different political-economic periods.

In the pre-Civil War South, most capital was concentrated in the hands of the cotton-producing slaveowners. From the beginning the economic interests of this class were fought for in the political arena through the vehicle of the Democratic Party. Under Jefferson the social base of this party remained fairly restricted. In many states in the South slaves were not the only people who were **disenfranchised**. Many free whites had no political voice because they could not meet the property qualifications required by state laws to make one eligible to vote.

In the Democratizing Party System period, the rise to power of the **Jacksonian Democrats** heralded a new tactic on the part of the slaveholders to broaden their social base. Their aim was to influence small farmers by appealing to a common interest in land and expansion. On this basis, the Democratic Party found adherents among yeoman farmers in the North. But its most important allies in the North were the urban financiers.

A number of Northern merchants and commercial people made their wealth from the triangular trade in slaves, rum, and foodstuffs between Africa, the West Indies, and North America. When the trade in slaves was outlawed in 1808, more and more of the wealth accumulated by this economic class went into other ventures. These included financing new slave-breeding plantations in the border states, bankrolling cotton producers, and speculating in land.

They were a new type of banker because they had never been dependent upon industry. They had grown on the basis of super-usury. Rather than growing through industrial production, this group matured on the slaughter of the Indians and the subsequent land speculations, upon the funding of the slave expeditions, and the looting of the public treasury. Unfettered by organic ties with any particular industry, their impulse was to scour the world for areas within which to utilize the mountain of investment capital that seemed to magically reproduce itself faster than it could be invested.[14]

Clearly, the only **protectionism** this section of capital favored was protection for the cotton industry. But for a long time there was no significant world competition in cotton.

The merchants, commercial people, and small manufacturers of the North and South had different problems and concerns. They were very sensitive to competition from manufactured imports and so favored strong tariffs and protectionist policies. Their economic interests were represented in the political arena through the **Federalist Party** in the Experimental Party System period.

In the Democratizing Party System period the Federalists were transformed into the **National Republicans** and later into the **Whig Party**. The Whigs constituted the main political opposition to the Democrats during this period. But—just as industrial capital was weaker then slave capital—so the Whigs were politically weaker than the Democrats.

It is important to note that the Whigs were organized across the national lines of North and South and represented a fairly homogeneous economic class in both nations. The composition of the Democratic Party was very different. It included the two sections of capital represented by the financiers of Philadelphia, New York, and Boston and by the Southern slaveholders; it also incorporated many farmers (in alliance with the planters) and many urban laborers in the North (in alliance with the financiers).

Labor's interests were in opposition to the economic interests of the manufacturers and merchants, who not only exploited labor in the production process but also were protectionists. **Protectionism** meant higher costs for essentials needed by the working class, and it also meant greater costs for planters who had a strong trading relationship with England, the main international buyer of cotton. Higher cotton-producing costs also meant lower profits for the big-city financiers of the North. Thus, common opposition to the emerging industrialists provided the basis for the unity of labor, farmers, planters, and financiers in the Democratic Party. This was the historical origin of **coalition politics** in the Democratic Party.

The earliest manifestation of this "unholy alliance" of labor, finance, and slavery was the establishment of the Virginia-New York Alliance between the Southern leaders of the Democratic Party and the infamous Tammany Hall political machine. The Tammany machine was promoted by leading New York financiers to organize and control the **immigrant labor** population beginning to pour into that port city.

> In [the] summer of 1791 Jefferson's skill as an adroit politician was demonstrated by his "botanizing trip" up the Hudson River. At that time he and James Madison went ostensibly on a botanical excursion, but actually for the purpose of forming political alliances in New York, where Governor George Clinton, the Livingston clan, and Aaron Burr, the manipulator of the St. Tammany Society of New York City, were opposed to the Federalist administration. In 1792 Virginia, North Carolina, Georgia, and New York voted for George Clinton for Vice-President instead of for John Adams. Thus began the Virginia-New York Alliance, which has played such a significant role in the rise of the Republican and Democratic parties.[15]

It should be noted that in Jefferson's day the Democratic Party was first called the Republican or **Democratic-Republican Party**, which is not the same Republican Party as today.

In the first two political-economic periods this party structure served two purposes for the capitalists in the Democratic Party. It gave them a farmer-labor base sufficient to overwhelm the political parties of industrial capital, and it also kept labor tightly tied to the leadership of capital. Already in the pre-Civil War period the common opposition of slaveholders and labor to industrial capital made the abandonment of the Democratic Party a risky venture for labor because a split vote would open the way to electoral victory for the Whigs.

Even during the Civil War, when the Southern Democrats were depicted by the **Republican Party** as traitors, the loyalties in the North to the Democratic Party were hard to break because of labor's fear of political domination by industrialists. The Democrats threatened to win the 1862 mid-term election and actually reduced the Republican advantage in the House of Representatives from sixty-two to only twenty-seven seats.[16]

The Civil War and Republican agitation on the **slavery question** did weaken the Democratic Party over the long term. Industrial capital—especially railroad capital—was growing in strength before the war. The full development of the economy on this new basis required the elimination of the still formidable opposition of the slave-holding Democrats. Since slavery was the economic foundation of Southern political power, abolishing slavery would break the political opposition to railroad capital. But slavery could not be abolished unless the South was conquered, and that meant raising an army willing to fight the South. The problem faced by the Republican industrialists was how to turn Northern workers and farmers away from the Democratic Party and convince them to follow the Republicans into battle.

What was needed was an **ideological issue** which made economic sense and which would effectively win over the "hearts and minds" of labor to the struggle against the South. That issue was slavery.

After the 1857-1858 economic collapse everyone knew the old economy was in deep trouble. The Republicans presented industrial solutions but said that the South stood in the way of progress for labor. They pointed out to farmers that the Southern planters were manipulating the terms under which new territories were brought into the Union. These terms favored the expansion of slave plantation lands to the disadvantage of independent farmers seeking their own land. Through this campaign, the abolitionist Republicans succeeded in splitting the Democratic Party in the 1860 elections and came to power as a **minority party**.

Thus, the first way in which the Republican Party of industrial capital worked the Southern question to its advantage was by agitating against the South as a roadblock to progress. In so doing, the Republicans brought many farmers and a section of the working class under their wing. But they remained a minority party after the war. With the cessation of hostilities they feared that Democrats in the North and South might join again in common opposition to the overbearing policies of railroad and industrial capital. These were years of the most blatant corruption in U.S. history as railroad capital repeatedly **bribed** its way into political office.

To further hamstring the Democrats, the Republicans developed other devices. They proposed changing the constitutional basis for representation in Congress so that the strength of the Southern Democrats would be permanently reduced.[17] In the end they settled upon the **military occupation** of the South as a means for keeping Southern Democrats out of office. As a result, Republican **Reconstruction governments** dominated the South from the end of the war to 1877. But the intermediate crisis of 1873-1877 forced the Republicans to shift tactics in order to maintain control of government. As Du Bois noted:

> The panic of 1873 changed, too, the history of the South. Already, in 1870, the Republicans had lost their two-thirds majority in Congress, and in 1874, for the first time in twenty years, the Democrats had a majority in the House of Representatives. They looked forward confidently to controlling the nation in 1875....
>
> The system of capital and private profit [was] smashed in 1873, and all property and investment were in dire danger;

labor was at the edge of starvation, and democracy and universal suffrage could function only through revolution.[18]

In short, railroad capital was in danger of losing its control over labor as a result of the crisis. Labor was voting more and more Democratic, but the old power of Southern slave capital in the Democratic Party had been abolished and was no longer available to control labor within the Democratic Party. It appeared that **revolutionary conditions** might be at hand. In fact, this was more appearance than reality. The disputed 1876 election between the Democratic candidate Tilden and the Republican candidate Hayes marked a shift in Republican tactics for manipulating the Southern question to its advantage and keeping control of labor.

The Two-Party System Since Reconstruction

To understand the 1876 shift in tactics by the Republican Party with regard to its Southern strategy, it is necessary to understand some of the history and class character of the Whigs before the Civil War and of the Southern Democrats after the war. An excellent summary of this question is available in Chapter Two of C. Vann Woodward's **Reunion and Reaction** (1951), subtitled "The Compromise of 1877 and the End of Reconstruction." Before the rise of the Republican Party in the 1850s, the **Whig Party** represented manufacturing interests in both the Northern and Southern nations. Perhaps the most famous of all Whigs was Henry Clay of Kentucky, the architect of numerous compromises over tariffs and questions of slavery. Southern Whigs were sometimes slave owners themselves but many—especially those in border states—were agreeable to a program of **compensated emancipation**, which was Lincoln's original position.

The developing national conflict between North and South ultimately proved more decisive than the cross-national class alliance among Whigs. The **Southern Whigs**, whose economic activities were unavoidably tied up with the whole cotton system, finally had no recourse but to enter the Democratic Party in the South as tensions between the two nations mounted. In the North the Whigs linked up with the Free Soil Party and the Abolitionists to form the **Republican Party**. Thus, the slavery issue split the Whigs along national lines.

After the war the Southern "Whig Democrats" were able to move into positions of power in the Democratic Party apparatus throughout the South while the Northern occupation armies suppressed the political activity of the recalcitrant planters. The **Southern Whig Democrats** would have liked to rejoin their Northern counterparts in the Republican Party. But so long as the Republicans remained identified in the South as the "party of the Negro people" it would have been impossible to shift the mass of Southern whites who fought against the North and in defense of slavery into the Republican Party.

Meanwhile the Northern financiers in the Democratic Party were buying into cotton and supplying badly needed capital to the manufacturers and commercial people represented by the Southern Whig Democrats. In a parallel political fashion, links were re-established between the Democratic Party organs in the North and South, but with the purse-strings controlled by the **Northern Democrats** (as they are to this very day). Thus, the nationalist-minded industrial class in the South became locked into the Democratic Party in alliance with the same financiers formerly aligned with the slave-holding planters.

In the North during Reconstruction the Republican Party pursued a policy of "waving the bloody shirt," a policy calculated to depict the South as a constant threat to the North, to Northern industrial policy, and to the new prosperity of Northern workers. In this way—and with reliance on the military-supported Republican governments in the Reconstruction South—the Republican Party held the workers' allegiance in the North and controlled the South. For sixteen years (1861-1877) political life in this country was conducted under conditions of **martial law**. For fourteen of those years the minority Republican Party had artificial control of the Presidency, the House, and the Senate.

The 1873-1877 crisis threatened to shatter Republican control because of the defection of labor from the Republican camp. To make matters worse the Democratic candidate, Samuel Tilden of New York City, was actually elected president in 1876, portending the rise to power of the New York City financiers. But it was a premature victory, and Tilden never took office.

Railroad capital still had some important political assets which it quickly cashed in to regain control. First, the former Whigs in the Northern Republican Party challenged the electoral votes for Tilden from several Southern states still under Northern military rule. Then they sought out the former Whigs in the Southern Democratic Party and made them a deal. The South would get railroads as part of a new infrastructure to support the rebuilding of the Southern nation's economy. In turn the Southern Whig Democrats had to help form an **electoral commission** in Congress favorable to the Republican challenge. The deal succeeded and the Republican candidate, Rutherford B. Hayes, was certified the winner and became president. Eventually the South got its railroads but they were organized and run to the benefit of Northern industrialists seeking access to the colonized Southern market.

Thus, the Northern Whig Republicans and the Southern Whig Democrats re-established political contact and entered into another long-term working relationship. From 1875 to 1933 there were twenty-nine different sittings of Congress, but during only fourteen of those did the Republican Party control the Presidency, the House, and the Senate. The character of the party as a true **minority party** incapable of holding the labor vote was clear, but the Republicans were able to legislate on the basis of their relationship with the Southern Whig Democrats who saw eye-to-eye with them on **industrial policy**. Thus, labor could vote Democratic and the Solid South would counter that vote by uniting with industrial capital. This is the same alignment which has enabled President Reagan to pass his anti-labor programs in the predominantly Democratic House of Representatives today.

In this way the power of the financiers was held at bay until the 1930s. But the ascendancy of the Republican Party could last only so long as industrial capital and railroad capital were stronger than bank capital in the economic arena. That economic strength provided the basis for cutting deals with nationalist Southern Democrats by promising them **internal improvements** in exchange for political support. With the 1930s depression that strength collapsed and it became the money power in the North that held the upper hand in dealing with the Southern Whig Democrats.

The **Solid South** was instrumental in implementing the New Deal program of the Northern financiers.

> [T]he South figured largely and indeed vitally in Roosevelt's political destinies. Most important of all, had it not been for Southern support, he would never have been nominated for President in 1932 and thus would never have reached the White House. It was Southern leadership in Congress that enacted the New Deal program and subsequently supplied to the President the requisite margin of votes to pass defense measures in the late thirties and early forties.[19]

Another historian adds:

> And on international affairs he retained their support, with few exceptions, to the very end.[20]

Roosevelt clearly indicated the centrality of Southern congressional support to the success of his programs when he said:

> "I've got to get legislation passed by Congress to save America. Southerners, by reason of the seniority rule in Congress, are chairmen or occupy strategic places on most of the Senate and House committees."[21]

As in the previous Republican-dominated period, the basis for holding the allegiance of the conservative Southern Democrats was the question of **internal improvements**.

Certain special Southern factors tied these Congressional leaders to President Roosevelt long after their first enthusiasm had dwindled.... [Most] important, the Roosevelt measures represented a giant, nation-wide cornucopia from which federal aid poured into the desperately Depression-ridden South. Distressing though this aid was to many of the Southern elite, Southern politicians concerned themselves more with channeling, rather than stemming, the flow. They did not want to join Republicans in curtailing it altogether.[22]

Of course, the possibility still existed that temporary alliances of the Republicans and the Southern Democrats could be put together on specific issues directly beneficial to both Northern and Southern industrial capital. However, V.O. Key, author of the famous **Southern Politics in State and Nation** (1949) described this relationship as much less important than in previous times.

Commonly a southern Senator is caricatured as a frock-coated, long-maned, and long-winded statesman of the old school who conspires in the cloakroom with Republicans to grind down the common man. He is supposed in return to receive generous campaign contributions from Wall Street as well as kudos from the conservative columnists who praise him as a constitutional scholar, a man of statesmanlike vision, and an embodiment of the virtues of the Founding Fathers. While there is in all this enough truth to embarrass good southern Democrats, the report of Southern Democratic-Republican congressional coalition has been not a little exaggerated.[23]

Unfortunately for the labor movement in the year of 1947, the existence of such an alliance was all too real if only temporary. It was on the basis of such a liaison that the infamous **Taft-Hartley Act** was passed. Hartley—himself a Republican—had high praise for the anti-labor complicity of Southern Democrats in both the House and Senate.

[T]he Labor-Management Relations Act of 1947 was as nearly a bipartisan measure as ever passed the Congress. Democrats and Republicans joined forces in the enactment of this legislation. And, as we all know, **only the votes of the southern members of President Truman's own party made possible its success.**[24] [emphasis added]

Hartley continued by lauding the key Southern Democrats on the House Committee on Education and Labor.

> Graham A. Barden, of North Carolina, ex-chairman of the old House Committee on Education.... served on the old House Labor Committee. Graham Barden is one of the finest southern gentlemen ever to serve in the House of Representatives; he had nothing but contempt for the labor racketeer and the professional union agitator. Most of the credit for placing the Taft-Hartley law above partisan politics goes to Graham Barden.
> Another southerner on the Committee was Representative O.C. Fisher, of Texas. Representative Fisher had long been opposed to the policies of the Democratic majority on the old Labor Committee. For many years he had joined with other southern Democrats in opposition to a permanent Fair Employment Practices Commission, to extensions of the Wage-Hour Act, and to other "liberal" and social aims of the New Deal. Fisher was to join with Graham Barden in uniting southern Democrats in support of my bill....
> Two other southern Democrats also joining with the Republican majority in writing the Taft-Hartley Act were John Wood, of Georgia, and Wingate Lucas, of Texas.[25]

And in the Senate:

> Senator Byrd, a Democrat, had taken the lead among the southern Democrats who gave their support to the Taft bill.[26]

The passage of the Taft-Hartley Act over the veto of a Democratic president suggested the beginning of a new period of rule by the political representatives of industrial capital in the North and South in reaction against much of the New Deal legislation promised to labor by the representatives of bank capital. However, the Eisenhower era was short lived. Bank capital remained formidable but found it advantageous to leave the Taft-Hartley Act in place. The Kennedy-Johnson alliance of Northern finance and Southern industry foretold the rejuvenation of the New Deal political coalition within the Democratic Party. Kennedy brought with him the labor vote, especially the **ethnic vote** in the Northeast, and Johnson—an old Roosevelt man from the 1930s—delivered the South. The means for doing the latter was the tried-and-true promise of **internal improvements**.

> During the campaign Johnson . . . held most of the South in line by the lures and threats best portrayed in a fanciful story a newsman told James A. Michener. After expressing sympathy for the state leaders' problems with the platform, Kennedy's Catholicism, and the civil rights movement, "Good Ol' Lyndon" would remind them that if defeated he and Kennedy would remain in the Senate: ". . . and, Senator Buford and Senator Baxby, I just don't see how, if your defection is the cause of our defeat, you're ever going to get one little old bill through that Senate. Governor Beauregard, you say you have to have that new airport and you want to keep the Army base down here. How do you think you're going to get such bills through the Senate if Mr. Kennedy and I are sitting there solely because you didn't produce the vote that would have elected us?"[27]

Since then, most Democratic **presidential tickets** have reflected this North-South axis and so have many of the Republican tickets. After Kennedy-Johnson there was Johnson-Humphrey (the Minnesotan having been a student of Southern politics himself as a graduate student at Louisiana State

University). The 1968 Nixon-Agnew victory was a triumph for the Southern strategy of the Republican Party.[28] Then came Carter-Mondale followed by Reagan-Bush (with Bush being touted as a Texan).

These contests highlight the main features of the **two-party system** in the United States since the period of the Democratizing Party System. The form of the Democratic Party has remained relatively constant over the years although its specific social composition has changed in a few ways. Before the Civil War it constituted an alliance of slave capital and Northern investment capital, with the former in the lead. Industrial capital in the Whig Party—North and South—played the loyal opposition. The **national struggle** between the North and the South resulted in the replacement of slave capital with Southern industrial capital in the Democratic Party, with the Northern financiers taking the dominant position in that party. However, they were still weaker than the new industrialists in the Northern-based Republican Party. The turn of the century brought an internal shift in power in the Republican Party from railroad capital to industrial capital based in manufactures. The New Deal Party System period marked the rise of the financiers in the Democratic Party to predominance over even these Republican industrialists.

The two-party system is, therefore, the form through which the leading sections of **capital** have historically fought for political leadership and control of the state apparatus in the United States. But the two-party system also reflects the relationship between the Northern and the Southern nations. The Civil War fixed this relationship as one of Northern dominance. Since then the struggle within capital has essentially been between Northern industrialists and Northern financiers, with Southern industrialists almost totally dependent on one or the other. Thus the South has become a political pawn in advancing the fortunes of different sections of Northern capital. This is clearly reflected in the development of a **Southern strategy** within each of the two major parties.

This is a struggle with serious implications for the interests of labor. Whichever section of capital can hold the allegiance of the

Southern Democrats has the lever to force labor into line behind its policies. For the Democrats, who have traditionally had the labor vote, control of the South means being able to make big promises to labor on the basis of Southern control of legislation. Thus, labor has been kept from any independent political action and held firmly in the Democratic camp.

But there are contradictions between the financiers and Southern industrialists in the Democratic Party just as there are between the financiers and Northern industrialists in the Republican Party. Consequently, there is some commonality of interests between industrialists in the Republican and Southern Democratic parties. This is most evident in the alliances struck between Republicans and Southern Democrats over labor issues. When the Republicans hold sway over Southern Democrats, the latter are used not as a means to **bribe** labor into allegiance but as a stick with which to **force** it into line.

Naturally this relationship is most likely to assert itself in times of economic crisis when industrial capital is hurt by falling profits. That is when industrialists look to labor to bear the brunt of the crisis by accepting cuts in real wages and other reductions in the standard of living in order to enhance **capital accumulation**. This was the essence of Eisenhower's policies during the post-World War II crises, of Nixon's freeze policies during the crisis of the early 1970s, and of Reagan's policies in the 1980s. The political result is that labor is drawn into the political arena in its own defense. But if labor shows any signs of independent political activity, this can be co-opted. As a crisis subsides, the financiers can make new concessions to Southern industry, win back the cooperation of the Southern Democrats, and regain control of the labor movement.

Unfortunately, this historical lesson is not understood by "progressive" leaders within the Democratic Party and the labor movement today. This is revealed in the politics of two closely allied leaders, William Winpisinger of the International Association of Machinists and former Democratic Congressman Michael Harrington of the Democratic Socialists of America. Harrington has even written about how to construct a new political alignment (with participation by labor) appropriate to a new period of economic expansion based on high technologies. The title of his most recent book designates the 1980s as a **Decade of Decision** for labor. He couldn't be more right about that. But what is the political solution he prescribes for labor?

Harrington correctly shows that labor—including "white collar" workers who are often not any better off than blue collar workers—is the most significant social sector in the United States. He points out that most blacks are located in this labor force. Therefore, two of the main components of the old New Deal Coalition—**labor** and **blacks**—are subsumed under the rubric of labor. A third element of that old coalition—the urban **liberals**—re-emerges in Harrington's writings as a "New Class" of liberal activists who matured in the New Left political battles of the 1960s. Harrington concludes:

> There is, then, another stratum in the society, not part of the working class, but with a basis for making an alliance with the working class. That possible coalition is the basis for political hope on the democratic Left during the next ten to twenty years.[29]

What Harrington wants is a "new" New Deal Coalition within the Democratic Party. In his view this coalition will give the labor movement all the political clout and independence it needs to secure its own interests. What he ignores is that every ruling coalition of Democrats in U.S. history has also included two other elements: Northern **financiers** and the **Solid South**. Such a coalition cannot succeed without them or the Democratic Party would be split and easily defeated by the Republicans. Any politician who claims that some facsimile of the New Deal Coalition can be reorganized within the Democratic Party today must ultimately admit that labor will have to join hands with both financiers and Southern Democrats to accomplish this. And that means that once again labor would be prey to the anti-labor **Dixiecrats** in Congress. There can be no such coalition in which labor is in control; it is an illusion that the Democratic Party is the vehicle for achieving labor's interests.

The **two-party system** in the United States is in reality a vicious triangle of struggle among "conservative" industrial capital and "liberal" bank capital in the imperialistic North and opportunistic industrial capital in the colonized South. Each section of capital looks out for its own interests. Because of the economically and politically controlled South, labor gets caught in the middle. This is the meaning of part of the **general formula for political rule** in the United States: i.e., whoever controls the South can control labor, and whoever controls labor can control the state. The central problem facing the labor movement has been how to break out of this bind.

5.

The Color Question in the South

In a recent interview on William F. Buckley's television program **Firing Line**, Steven Millner, Assistant Professor of Sociology and Southern Studies at the University of Mississippi, had some interesting comments on the commonalities of black and white **culture** in the South. He was talking about the regional cultural impact of Nashville's popular WLAC radio station.

> If you look at Southern blacks, they share very much with Southern whites. They share a legacy of listening to WLAC at late night, and that's the kind of cultural orientation that is completely foreign to blacks from the West and from the North.... WLAC was a courting station. People listened to LAC as they courted, whether they were black or white, at two o'clock in the morning—to a regional station that had a large following among all Southerners.... It had appeal to Southerners who liked country music, who liked blues, and who could detect quite easily the strong parallels between those two musical styles.... The beat is the same, and the music was basically apolitical. Since it was apolitical, whites and blacks could both relate to it.[1]

Another guest on the program, James C. Cobb, Professor of History at Old Miss, described the live political question which still affects the South.

[R]ace relations in the South now stand on a basis that was certainly peculiar within the United States—an historical basis of the plantation and of a rigid caste system, a system of political disenfranchisement that has yet by any means to disappear. And it's one thing to say, "Yes, there was discrimination, there was segregation in Northern cities," but there was also going to work and earning a paycheck and escaping into a certain amount of anonymity within what was still a discriminatory society; and the differences for a Southern black attempting to do the same thing I think would still prove to be very significant now. Of course it's true that blacks have returned—reverse migration—to the South. There is obviously a perception that the South is a much improved place to live for blacks, and I'm certain that it is. But...despite the end of de jure segregation and the dismantling of a lot of the caste system, one still observes a peculiarly Southern set of race relations.[2]

This question of the color line in the South is relevant to understanding the possibilities for and dangers of a new political alignment in which Northern labor is drawn into another alliance with reactionary Southern Democrats. If control of the Northern labor movement depends on the existence of the Solid South, then the Solid South depends on the control of Southern labor on the basis of the **color question**. In this regard a century-old observation still gets to the heart of the problem for Northern labor.

In the United States of North America, every independent movement of the workers was paralyzed so long as slavery disfigured a part of the Republic. Labor cannot emancipate itself in the white skin where in the black it is branded.[3]

Du Bois later called the color question "the Blindspot of American political and social development"[4] and concluded that the equality of white and black labor is "the most stupendous labor problem of the twentieth century" and the key to "transcending the problem of Labor and Capital."[5]

The question of the **color line** in the South and its impact on labor is therefore not just an abstract **moral dilemma** confronting Northern and Southern labor. Yet this is how the question has been posed to labor since the founding of the Abolitionist movement. But no moral force or organization has been able to abolish the color line. In fact, it has taken new developments in the political economy of world capitalism to establish the conditions for uprooting color barriers in the South. Now the consequences of the color question—i.e., the control of the South and of Northern labor—are being exposed. The conditions for the independent political activity of labor are finally developing.

Basis of the Solid South

The previous chapter established that the basis for co-opting and controlling the political impulses of the Northern labor movement is control of the **Solid South**. To this point the existence of the tightly run Southern Democratic political machine has simply been assumed without explaining the basis for its seemingly permanent status in the political system of the United States. Indeed, it is easy to take the Solid South for granted because unlike any other political organization, its history is as old as the country itself. Except for temporary inroads into Southern political life—the pre-Civil War Whigs, the Republican Reconstruction governments, and a trend toward voting Republican in presidential elections today—the South has long been the bastion of the Democratic Party, especially at state and local levels.

The "dictatorship" of the Democratic Party in the South has been based on political control of Southern blacks, first by Southern planter capital and later by Southern industrial capital. This political stratagem is a legacy of slavery itself. Although the social status of blacks in Southern society has been reformed over the years, the character of every reform has been limited by the condition that control of the black vote be retained by the

Democratic Party. Consequently, another part of the **general formula** for maintaining political power is that control of the Southern black is the means for controlling the South.

This leads directly to the question of the **white workers** in the South who, in theory, could stand opposed to the Democratic Party machine of Southern capital. But the political control of Southern blacks—through slavery in the pre-Civil War periods, through segregation and disenfranchisement in the pre-New Deal periods, and through gerrymandering today—has historically given the Southern Democrats the means to control the Southern white worker as well. With control of the **black vote**, the Southern Democratic Party can appeal to the white worker with the same argument that the Northern Democrats (with control of the Southern wing of the party) use to co-opt the Northern labor vote: ally yourselves with us and you will derive the benefits of our controlled political base. Oppose us and we will all be weakened in the pursuit of our various interests.

Southern capital needs to present a solid front to the Northern Democrats and Republicans in bargaining for the best political and economic deals from each. Thus the Southern Democrats enter into opportunistic political alliances with one or the other section of Northern capital, the trade-off being the South's help in controlling the Northern labor movement. In the North the whole **labor movement** is made impotent by falling into league with the representatives of capital in hopes of using the Solid South to its class advantage. In a parallel sense, white workers in the South become impotent when they accept the leadership of Southern capital in hopes of using the tightly controlled black vote in their own interests. The real benefits of these alliances accrue to capital itself.

In the North labor remains politically subordinate to capital, the economic system is preserved, and the exploitation of labor by capital continues. Northern labor gets the impression that it is benefitting from this set-up, for the most technically advanced industries paying the highest wages are developed there while aging or less profitable industries are shifted south. In the South labor also remains subordinate to capital and is made the object of super-exploitation. By legal and extra-legal means, capital restricts blacks to the lowest-paying industries in the South while somewhat better jobs are reserved for whites. But the competition of lower-paid black labor for jobs serves as a drag on all wages in the Southern labor market. Thus the **value of labor power** in the Southern nation is held below its market value in the whole country. As a result Southern labor can be more profitably employed than Northern labor at the same work. Still, the Southern white worker gets the impression that his alliance with Southern capital brings certain benefits, at least relative to blacks.

Through this economic manipulation white loyalty to the Democratic Party with its controlled black base is reinforced. The forced control of Southern blacks and the co-optation of Southern whites form the basis of the solidly Democratic South. The manipulation of the color question in the South not only divides labor along a color line; it also becomes the lever for winning a section of that class to the program of capital: i.e., by representing capital's "particular interest as general" and its class "interest as the common interest of all the members of society."[6] Note that it is Southern capital which promotes the color question. White labor has merely succumbed to the siren song of self-interest inherent in the color question.

The appeals for the unity of Southern white labor with Southern capital are essentially nationalist appeals; i.e., they are based on the ideology of **nationalism**. This ideology claims that what is best for capital in a given nation is also best for labor. By accepting the nationalist leadership of capital, labor automatically subordinates itself and its whole future to the roller-coaster fortunes of the capitalist system. The use of nationalist appeals to promote the foreign policy interests of capital is well known. Whenever the government claims that "national security" is at stake, workers are called upon to enhance that security through military mobilization and war. A domestic variant of nationalism which blurs class interests and perpetuates the domination of capital is the appeal for labor to unite with capital against another section of society. In the Northern nation this takes the form of the financiers getting labor to line up with them against the industrialists. In the Southern nation it takes the form of the industrialists getting white workers to line up with them against blacks.

Factors in Southern Nationalism

Despite the historical success of nationalist appeals in uniting capital and labor in the North and in the South, the supposed benefits to labor are always temporary at best. The preservation of the capitalist system may be prolonged by thwarting the independent political power of labor. However, the inevitable crises of the capitalist system cannot be avoided.

In the North every critical crisis and many serious intermediate crises brought with them an upsurge in the political activity of the working class and direct confrontations with capital. Use of the Southern **political reserve** by capital has been crucial in directly repressing the working class movement (as the Republicans do in alliance with the Southern Democrats) or co-opting that movement (as the Northern Democrats do in alliance with the same Southern Democrats).

In the South the political situation in crises is different by virtue of the South's colonized status. Because of this status, the history of crises in the South since the Civil War has been characterized by the resurgence of **national movements**. In essence, each of these national movements has been—to borrow a chapter title from C. Vann Woodward's **Origins of the New South, 1877-1913**—a "Revolt Against the East," i.e., against the colonized status of the Southern labor market and especially against the superexploitation of black labor.

The national revolt in the South often takes contradictory forms as a result of the color line in Southern society. Thus, during crises the national movement among Southern white workers typically takes the form of a "struggle to equalize living standards with the North" with the "federal government as the chief enemy."[7] But crises also result in the periodic resurgence of the Negro people's movement for economic and political independence from the heavy hand of capital. Because of the color question, the Negro people's movement is directed more at Southern capital itself and repeatedly finds itself looking to the "enemy of its enemy" (i.e., the federal government) for help and protection.

Thus for the past 100 years we have seen a very strange political phenomenon. There is a national colonial question presented by the conversion of the Black Belt into a colony as a consequence of the Civil War. Within that struggle is the historic, centuries-old struggle of the black masses for equality. These two aspects of the struggle for national liberation are deeply intertwined and interdependent. The segregation, discrimination, and inequality of the blacks that is the result of the color factor in our history compels the black masses into a fight that appears to be separated from the general national movement of the colonial Black Belt as a whole which includes all the people there, regardless of color.

In summary, we are dealing with a national colonial question in the Black Belt. One political aspect is the struggle of the black masses for national liberation of the Black Belt in the form of the struggle for equality with their white counterparts, wherever they may be.

Another, often contradictory aspect is the struggle of the white masses for national liberation of the Black Belt as expressed in their struggle against the federal government and for wage and cultural parity with the North.[8]

Both of these movements are **political factors** in the actual struggle of Southern labor for independence from Southern capital and Northern imperialism. Despite their apparent contradictoriness, they are both sustained by the same drive for class interest and against colonial oppression. To adapt a phrase from an early proponent of the materialist conception of history, these factors "ultimately can both be related to the same course of economic development" in the South.[9]

It is the **color question** which has continually split the working class movement in the South and isolated these political factors from each other. If this split in the Southern working class were to be overcome, this would be a serious blow to the maintenance of the solid Democratic South, the workings of the two-party system in the United States, and therefore to the method of controlling the Northern labor movement.

In times of crisis these two factors do exhibit strong tendencies toward political unity, although such unity has ultimately always foundered on the agitation of the color question by the leaders of Southern capital. That is a tactic formulated in the latter's own class interest in order to maintain the "Solid South."

In turn, the solidly Democratic South is the bargaining chip for Southern capital to use in striking deals with dominant Northern capital. In return for economic concessions, the leaders of Northern capital get the "Solid South" as a reserve political strength for use in subduing the Northern labor movement. A second advantage is that the split labor movement in the South continues to make the South an excellent **economic reserve** for extending the profitable life of old industries.

Controlling the Southern Labor Movement

Every critical crisis in U.S. history has engendered a struggle between different sections of capital for political leadership. That is **one condition** of a revolutionary crisis. Crises also push the working class into spontaneous rebellion against their conditions of existence, and that creates the **second condition** of a revolutionary crisis. Because the United States is a multi-national state, a third manifestation of a revolutionary crisis must also be present for a class change in political leadership to become possible. That **third condition** is the impulse toward unity of action by both white and black workers in the South.

Since the onset of the antagonistic relationship between the white slave owner and the black slave in the Southern nation, there has been an unscientific tendency to represent the **Negro** people's movement as the only revolutionary movement in the South. In fact, it is merely the leading and most consistent of the two political factors comprising the movement against the domination of Northern capital and its Southern allies. Agitation of the color question has always been the lever in the South for crushing any unity of action of the black and white working masses, the former by force and the latter by co-optation to the side of force (i.e., capital). Historically the Ku Klux Klan, formed in 1866, has been the terrorist tool of Southern capital for isolating blacks in Southern society. Thus, it has appeared that the only real struggle for freedom and equality in the South is the resistance movement among blacks.

The fundamental class interests of the Southern white workers have always been tied to the interests of the black masses, while actions by white workers in support of capital have always betrayed those same class interests. There is no clearer expression of the self-recrimination among Southern whites for such self-betrayal than the guilt-wracked **national literature** of the South (Faulkner, Tennessee Williams, etc.). On the part of blacks there is a corresponding plaint represented in blues music, a transcendent feeling expressed in jazz, and the eternal hope for better things to come reflected in gospel music. The interests of black and white workers in the South have always been linked, and most people are aware of this either consciously or unconsciously, as reflected in **Southern culture**.

Likewise, political movements among Southern blacks have always reflected common black and white interests. Every instance of resistance to slavery—and there were many[10]—was an action directed against the same planter class which monopolized the best land in the South to the exclusion of the **poor white** dirt farmer. The continual need to expand the slave-based plantation system was the driving force behind this exclusion, so slavery drew strong opposition from whites as well. At the beginning of the Democratizing Party System period, "out of 143 emancipation societies in the U.S. in 1826, 103 were in the South, including 4 abolition papers (1819-28)."[11]

However, as in subsequent critical crises, when the impulses toward unity of black and white struggles emerged, Southern political leaders moved quickly to snuff them out.

The Southern states met abolitionist propaganda with regulatory or prohibitory laws. A Georgia code (1835) provided the death penalty for the publication of material tending to incite slave insurrections. Northern abolitionist editors and agents were expelled from the South. To the South Carolina legislature (1835) Governor McDuffie declared that "the laws of every community should punish this species of interference by death without benefit of clergy." At Charleston (29 July), a boatload of abolitionist tracts from New York impounded by the postmaster was seized by a mob and publicly burned. The Charleston postmaster, Alfred Huger, requested anti-slavery societies to discontinue their use of the mails; his appeal was rejected. When Huger's report reached Postmaster General Kendall, the latter replied that he had no official authority to bar abolitionist propaganda from the mails; unofficially he advised Southern postmasters to intercept such material, having already declared, "We owe an obligation to the laws, but a higher one to the communities in which we live."[12]

By agitation of the color question, backed up by force, the joint movement of whites and blacks against slavery was steadily crushed. But such a movement could not be killed because its roots still existed. In the crisis at the end of the Democratizing Party System period, it became clear to the representatives of independent white farmers (**yeomen**) that again their interests lay along the same lines as the slaves.

North Carolina produced three valiant critics of slavery during the last decade of the ante-bellum period.... The most significant opponent of slavery that the state nurtured was the writer Hinton Rowan Helper, a representative of the yeoman class of the Piedmont.

In 1857 Helper published in New York City **The Impending Crisis of the South**, in which he tried to show that the South was far inferior to the North in economic productivity and general civilisation as a result of the burden of slavery.... He also developed the view that the slaveholding oligarchy had conspired to keep the poor whites in a dependent, illiterate condition. With considerable accuracy he may be called the Karl Marx of the nonslaveholding whites whom he tried to arouse to a sense of class consciousness.... **The Impending Crisis** was published as a campaign document for the Republican Party, and it became a crime in the South to circulate it....

Although he was an immediate abolitionist, [Helper] hated the Negroes, whom he regarded as the competitors of the poor whites. Like the Georgia pamphleteer, John Jacobus Flournoy, Helper was a Negrophobe, a bitter expulsionist, urging the wholesale shipping of the Negroes to Africa.[13]

Thus the understanding of the commonality of interests of black and white workers remained limited, conditional, and subject to defeat by agitation on the color question.

The conviction of the Southern people in 1860 that slavery was justified... represent[ed] a striking victory of mass propaganda—one of the greatest in human history.[14]

Helper recognized that the only way the South could advance as a nation on a par with the North was by doing away with slavery and organizing the economy on the basis of free labor. Just as the slave wanted emancipation and land, so the poor white could not get land without the abolition of slavery. Their destinies were interlocked, and the roadblock to the advancement of each was the power of Southern planter capital. But the planters successfully played on the "threat" of uncontrolled black freedom to convince the poor white that the only way to get land was to support **ter-**

ritorial expansion into the Southwest (in the Mexican-American War of 1846-1848) and later to carry the Civil War to the North. The poor white clearly wanted land. He got it after the war—alongside the black **sharecropper**—and was rarely better off than his black neighbors.

The post-Civil War period of Reconstruction perpetuated the split in Southern labor. The Republican government in the victorious North used its occupation armies to enforce the election of Republican state governments and Republican congressmen from the South. The main political constituency of these governments and representatives was the freed blacks. The Republican objective was not to enhance the economic and political conditions of blacks per se, but to maintain control of the federal government for Northern railroad and industrial capital. So long as slavery existed, it was the Southern planters who had the means to inflate their representation in Congress. This was because the Constitution permitted each slave to be counted as three-fifths of a person in figuring **apportionment**, even though slaves could not vote. With emancipation, the South could actually have increased its weight in government because every free black was to be counted as one man with one vote. Thus the post-war power of Northern capital was threatened.

> When... the South went beyond reason and truculently demanded not simply its old political power but increased political power based on disfranchised Negroes, which it openly threatened to use for revision of the tariff, for the repudiation of the national debt, for disestablishing the national banks, and for putting the new corporate form of industry under strict state regulation and rule, Northern industry was frightened and began to move towards the stand which abolition-democracy had already taken; namely, temporary dictatorship, endowed Negro education, legal civil rights, and eventually even votes for Negroes to offset the Southern threat of economic attack.[15]

CONTROLLING THE SOUTHERN LABOR MOVEMENT 147

Reconstruction meant bringing the free black under the wing of the Republican Party for its own political advantage. The Southern Democrats, in turn, played up the "threat of Negro domination" to bring the poor whites under their wing.

The struggle between the capitalist leadership of the two nations extended beyond the war itself, but it was no longer a military struggle. Rather it became a struggle for the "legal" control of the federal state, and control of the free black became the key. Since the North had the upper hand in this struggle, Southern Democratic leaders fell back on the poor whites for a political base. Thus, Southern labor remained split in the Reconstruction period. Meanwhile Northern capital used its economic power to penetrate the Southern economy. Then it forced Southern capital into **dependence**. Most importantly, Northern and Southern ex-Whigs began to rebuild political contact even though they were concentrated in two different parties.

The struggle between Northern and Southern capital was finally put aside.

> When Northern and Southern employers agreed that profit was most important and the method of getting it second, the path to understanding was clear. When white laborers were convinced that the degradation of Negro labor was more fundamental than the uplift of white labor, the end was in sight.
>
> All that was necessary, then, was to satisfy Northern industry that the new combination in the South was essentially a combination which aimed at capitalistic exploitation on conventional terms. The result was the withdrawal of military support and the revolutionary suppression not only of Negro suffrage but of the economic development of Negro and white labor.
>
> It was not until after [this] period . . . that white labor in the South began to realize that they had lost a great opportunity, that when they united to disenfranchise the black laborer they had cut the voting power of the laboring class in two. White labor in the Populist movement of the eighties tried to realign

the economic warfare in the South and bring workers of all colors into united opposition to the employer.... They realized that it was not simply the Negro who had been disfranchised in 1876, it was the white laborer as well.[16]

Having no real political power, poor whites were forced into sharecropping too. Relegated to virtually the same position as the "free" black in the post-Civil War economy, the white Southern sharecropper found common cause with blacks during the next critical crisis in the 1890s. This was most evident in the affiliated actions of the white Southern Farmers Alliance and the Colored Farmers National Alliance.[17] In the political arena, Southern whites and blacks joined the Populist Party and jointly supported its candidates. As a result a legitimate movement developed in the South for independence from the conditions of **national oppression** enforced by the North.

Its attack was directed primarily, not against the planters, and...not even very definitely against the supply merchants, but against the railroads and two Yankee creations called the Money Power and the Cotton Exchange; its prevailing objective was the seizing of the national government for putting down these monsters....

[A]fter the Civil War... the tariff gang had now got a completely free hand. The South in the nineties, having to sell its [cotton] for the lowest price in history, was having to buy its wants at prices held to the very highest level that even the Yankee standard of living would bear—by far the highest level in the world. Which is in effect to say that a very great part of even such poor wealth as it could manage to create was being drained off to fatten the pockets of the masters of the North....

The great banking interests of New York were an integral, and in the last analysis probably the most essential, part of the tariff gang. And, for that matter, these banking interests were guilty of exploiting the South in other ways on their own private account, the whole system of cotton financing... being in large part simply a reflection of the terms imposed by them on Southern bankers and merchants or those persons in Yankeedom who supplied Southern bankers and merchants.[18]

At the heart of the **national inequality** of the South lay the status of Southern blacks. Lewis H. Blair, a Southern industrialist and veteran of the Civil War, returned to his native city of Richmond after the war to find it in total ruin. But he imagined that with the war behind them, Southerners would witness a new era of prosperity. Two decades later he realized that the South was in no better shape than at the end of hostilities. In 1889 he published his analysis of the social reasons for the South's subordination and found the following: that **the prosperity of the South was dependent upon the elevation of blacks.**

> There are many causes conspiring to the poverty or lack of prosperity of the South, the principal of which are the general prevalence of ignorance, a general disregard of human life, a general lack of economy and self denial; but great as these causes are, a greater and more far-reaching cause of all is the degradation of the Negro.... Like a malignant cancer which poisons the whole system, this degradation seems to intensify all the other drawbacks under which we labor. Thus general ignorance is intensified by the gross ignorance of all blacks and of the whites nearest them in social and financial condition; the general disregard of human life is intensified by the slight regard in which a Negro's life is held.... We may remove all the other hindrances to prosperity; the whites may become well educated; we may hold human life in scrupulous regard and may become models of economy and self-denial, but if the blacks are to be left to grovel in their present degraded condition, even then prosperity would be measurably in default, because the six million Negroes, remaining degraded, would prove an incubus upon the whites,

who would be in imminent danger of impoverishment by the thieving of such multitudes....

Although justice... demands that the whites elevate the Negroes, for in the light of morality we stand responsible for their welfare, their elevation will not be advocated on any such ground, nor on the ground of religion either, but simply on economic grounds....

That is a very hard doctrine, perhaps, but we must remember that facts themselves are hard things, and that they never think of accommodating themselves to either our desires or our fancies. We would like a more "comforting"... doctrine, did not reading, observation and experience show that morality and even religion are very poor advocates, unless they can show to their listeners that material benefit is on their side. Convinced therefore, as I must be that benefit is the only safe and sound ground to base an argument upon... I shall address my arguments to prove not only that the prosperity of the South will be increased by, but that it is dependent upon, the elevation of the Negro.[19]

While scrupulously avoiding any mention of abolishing **wage labor**, Blair perceived economic advantage for Southern industrial capital in abandoning agitation of the color question. By healing the rift in Southern labor, the Northern and Southern labor markets might be equalized and the South could become economically (and politically) competitive with the North. This was Southern industry's reaction to the South's colonized status going into the critical crisis of the 1890s.

The **Populist movement** among farmers also developed in reaction to these colonized conditions. But the leadership of this movement was soon captured by prominent Southern planters such as Ben Tillman, who were securely tied to—and compromised by their dependence on—Northern capital. The planters once again stirred up the color question, claimed that blacks threatened to take over the movement to the detriment of whites, turned white against black, led the Populists back into the

Democratic Party in 1896, and preserved the Solid South and the rule of capital.

All through the eighties and the early nineties the common whites may be said... to have been groping in some dim, obscure, and less than conscious fashion toward perception of their position in the Southern world and to have been gathering anger against it. That was one of the elements in the growth of the Farmer's Alliance movement, and the greatest Populist outbreak of the nineties in which the movement culminated: in the emergence upon the scene of the Southern demagogue as a type, with Ben Tillman of South Carolina as the first great exponent of the role.

And Ben Tillman himself was no poor white but a considerable landowner.... Nor was his dominant theme ever the plight of the tenants and the sharecroppers as such, but that of the cotton-grower in general.[20]

Thus, the character of the movement was shifted from its progressive potential for uniting whites and blacks to a conservative course in which blacks were segregated and disenfranchised and the separate interests of poor whites and capitalists obscured.

Still, the political fate of Southern whites remained entangled with that of Southern blacks. To pre-empt any future efforts at joint political action by blacks and whites, Southern blacks were effectively barred from voting by state **disenfranchisement laws** passed between 1895 and 1910 and segregated by **Jim Crow laws** passed between 1900 and 1915.[21]

The laws used against blacks were also used to strike dissident whites from the voting rolls. By 1924 the grip of the Southern Democratic Party machine was so complete that only 6 percent of the electorate voted in the presidential contest. When Senator Blease learned that Coolidge, the Republican candidate, had received just over one thousand votes in South Carolina, he exclaimed:

"I do not know where he got them. I was astonished to know that they were cast and shocked to know they were counted."²²

The economic fate of Southern white and black workers remained intertwined as well. The mass of workers were still **sharecroppers** although, as a result of the Jim Crow laws, some whites were granted the "privilege" of toiling in textile sweatshops from which blacks were excluded.²³ Once again, in the critical crisis of the 1930s, the common interests of these workers were reasserted and resulted in the formation of the Alabama Sharecroppers Union in 1931 and the Southern Tenant Farmers Union in 1934.

Although it was not the first attempt by sharecroppers to rebel against the viciousness of the plantation caste system, the organization of the Southern Tenant Farmers Union (STFU) was to have far-reaching effect in bringing the "plight of the sharecropper" to the nation's consciousness. Subjected to continuous harassment and intimidation by the landed gentry and their hired lawmen, the union nevertheless continued to grow in both membership and mass appeal. Throughout the '30's and into the early war years it spread to six southern states. Stubbornly maintaining its union structure despite rebuffs by both the CIO and AFL, it became a mass movement—a movement that people joined with the enthusiasm they normally saved for their religion, a movement that gave common people the means to organize and fight for the right to live decent and productive lives.²⁴

The STFU was notable for its combined white and black constituency, but the spread of this kind of united activity among agricultural workers and workers in other industries was severely limited by the **chauvinism** of the big Northern unions. For a long time both the AFL and CIO balked at helping to organize white sharecroppers because it meant they would have to organize blacks as well. The work of the STFU remained restricted because of implicit AFL and CIO policies not to organize blacks. Only when Southern blacks moved North in record numbers during World War II to fill the labor shortage in Northern industries did Northern unions come to accept blacks in their ranks.[25] Another factor limiting black/white unity was the terror used against Southern blacks to keep them from joining the STFU movement. The 1930s saw a tremendous upsurge in this sort of terror in the South.[26] Meanwhile, the credit structure of Southern agriculture was revamped through such acts as the Agricultural Adjustment Act of 1933. This saved the operations of big agribusinesses in the South and made them more reliant than ever on Northern finance.[27] Unemployment insurance and other such **relief projects** dulled the revolutionary edge of the movement among bankrupt sharecroppers.[28]

Thus the economic, social, and political structure of the South in the Industrial Party System period was carried over into the New Deal Party System period, with the solidly Democratic South becoming an essential building block in the New Deal coalition. The liberalized democracy afforded to Northern workers by the Democratic Party had its firm foundation in an opportunistic coalition with an overtly **fascist** Democratic Party organization in the South. Here is how a 1938 editorial in the Charleston **News and Courier** described this political creed.

> Again let it be... clearly understood that were the **News and Courier** a democratic newspaper, if it believed in democracy as President Roosevelt believes in it... it would demand that every white man and woman and every black man and woman in the South be protected in the right to vote. It would demand the abolition of all "Jim Crow" laws, of all drawing of the color line by law. That is democracy. But the **News and Courier** is not a democrat. It fears and hates democratic government....
>
> In South Carolina, the Democratic party has been, so far as the Negro vote is concerned, a Fascist party, and that is why the **News and Courier** "cooperates" with it.[29]

On the basis of the color question in the South, the solidly Democratic South was maintained. And on the basis of the Solid South the financial interests in the North have been able to keep control of the Northern labor movement and hold it in the Democratic Party.

New Conditions in the South

There has not been another upsurge among black and white workers in the South until the recent crisis. Some of the new manifestations of this tendency toward class unity have been the **union drives** among black and white workers in Southern textile mills (especially at J.P. Stevens plants)[30] and unified strike activity by over twenty thousand black and white steelworkers at the largest industrial facility in the South—the Newport News shipbuilding yards in Virginia—in 1979-1980. In 1982 the AFL-CIO targeted the growing industrial city of Houston on the fringe of the old cotton belt for its largest labor organizing drive in years.

In reaction, the divisive work of **white supremacy** is also mounting in both legal and extra-legal arenas. The open activity of the KKK and the American Nazi Party is increasing across the South, as evidenced in the formation of guerrilla training camps and the assassination of white and black union organizers in Greensboro, North Carolina in 1979.[31] At the same time, a concerted effort has emerged among conservative Southern Democrats to roll back civil rights won during the 1950s and 1960s, end desegregation programs, and weaken voting rights for all Southerners.[32]

If in this critical crisis blacks can be forced into isolation from Southern whites, the consequence would be a significant weakening of their objectively common struggle. But some significant new conditions which have developed in the South since World War II make such a split more difficult to foment than ever before. If this split cannot be revived in such a way as to maintain the grip of the Democratic Party in the South, then the continued operation of the **two-party system** to the advantage of capital and to the detriment of labor could collapse.

The objective character of production is more and more creating the conditions for a unified movement of blacks and whites in a common cause against Wall Street imperialism. We cannot overstate the importance of this motion. It is the foundation for the revolution.[33]

The origins of these new conditions are to be found in the changed position of the United States in the world economy as a result of World War II. Although it was an important power before the war, only after the war did the United States become the leading world power in terms of economic, political, and military might. This new stature was achieved coincident with the rise to political power of the **financial section of capital** in the United States. This grouping has dominated the formulation of domestic and foreign policy ever since.

Victory in the war brought new problems and new prospects for the expansion of bank capital. The possibilities for new investments depended on increasing the capacity of American industry to meet the needs of **reconstruction** in Europe. In the colonies and former colonies of the ruined European powers, the possibilities for major new bank investments depended on the ability of the United States to implement a controlled **de-colonization process** and then to increase capital goods and food production to supply the wants of industry and labor in these new markets. Finally, in relation to the growing number of socialist countries which were supporting revolutionary changes in the same former colonies, the possibilities for the investment of bank capital depended on the ability to create a large, permanent **military sector of the economy** to restrict socialist advances. All of these problems necessitated a vast expansion of the productive capacity of the economy.

Since the South was the major economic reserve of the United States, the solution to these industrial problems involved heavy reliance on the South. The shift of chemicals, military production and other manufactures into the South opened the way for the expansion of other industries in the North. This was a typical trend in previous political-economic periods, especially after a new sector of capital had established its dominance through war and legislation and then encountered crises of its own making. And so it was in the post-World War II years: "Ever since the recession of 1948 there has been an increasing flight of industry from the North to the South."[34]

The industrialization of the South on the scale required by the problems of reconstruction, de-colonization, and militarization was no simple matter. It was such a massive undertaking that it soon became clear it could not be carried out using white workers alone. The proletarianization of white and black **sharecroppers** was imperative in order to provide a large enough workforce. President Truman noted the problem and the implications for the South as early as 1947.

> One of the principal economic problems facing us and the rest of the world is achieving maximum production and continued prosperity. . . .
>
> Discrimination imposes a direct cost upon our economy through the wasteful duplication of many facilities and services required by the "separate but equal" policy. That the resources of the South are sorely strained by the burden of a double system of schools and other public services has already been indicated. Segregation is also economically wasteful for private business.[35]

The dislocation of sharecroppers began with the introduction of the mechanical cotton picker and thus the **mechanization** of cotton agriculture.[36]

> During the 1940s the number of Negro farm operators in the South declined 18 percent from 680,000 to 559,000. The real crunch, however, came later, and coincided with Wall Street's realization after the Korean war that it had to solve

once and for all the problem of industrializing the South. Thus in the 1950s the number of black farm operators in the South was cut by more than half, and in the 1960s declined 66 percent from 266,000 to only 90,000. White farmers in the South, though not hit quite so badly, fell in number from about 2.3 million in 1940 to just 1.1 million thirty years later. All told, this marked a tremendous **proletarianization** of both the black and white laboring masses in the South in the post-Korean war period.[37]

This was only the first step in the transformation of the South. Mechanization may have created plenty of workers for industry, but **segregation laws** still made it impossible for black workers to get industrial jobs alongside whites.

[I]t soon became clear that it would be impossible to fully exploit the labor in the South so long as the law—written and unwritten—effectively kept the Negro out of industry. Thus, there unfolded a second edition of the tragedy of reconstruction. The moral force, the physical energy, the democratic aspirations of the Negro people were cynically directed by the Kennedy and Johnson administrations to achieve the goal of the financiers. That goal was to create the legal and social conditions to proletarianize the Negro. One by one the laws of segregation were struck down. Also struck down were the scores of Negro leaders who understood the trap into which the Negro movement was being led. No one can doubt the economic and social advance of a large section of the Negro people as a result of the movement of the 1960's. But the historic result was the drawing into industry and industrial exploitation of the millions of Negro toilers who heretofore had been excluded from the industrial life of the South.[38]

That is a brilliant summary of the dual character of the Civil Rights Movement: i.e., as a movement of the most oppressed section of the Southern working class away from the grip of capital as maintained in one period and into a different grip suited to a different period. It is a good example of how Northern capital manipulates the **Negro people's movement** in the South to its own advantage.

Southern white workers also gained from the achievements of the Civil Rights Movement. **Integration** paved the way for more industrialization and jobs for blacks. But whites got jobs too—better jobs—and black leaders who challenged the existence of economic, social and political advantages for white workers were physically eliminated and replaced by less truculent black leaders. The old myth of "separate but equal" was transformed into the reality of integrated but unequal. But the integration of Southern workers in the workplace has set in motion a revolution in labor unity.

The International Significance of the South

The conditions which transformed the South developed as a result of World War II. Before the war the Roosevelt administration balked at supporting any significant social changes in the South. But after the war, President Truman's administration was unavoidably confronted with the economic and political necessity of Southern **social reform**.

> Our position in the postwar world is so vital to the future that our smallest actions have far-reaching effects.... Our foreign policy is designed to make the United States an enormous, positive influence for peace and progress throughout the world. We have tried to let nothing, not even extreme political differences between ourselves and foreign nations, stand in the way of this goal. But our domestic civil rights shortcomings are a serious obstacle.
> We cannot escape the fact that our civil rights record has been an issue in world politics. The world's press and radio are full of it.... We and our friends have been, and are, stressing our achievements. Those with competing

philosophies have stressed—and are shamelessly distorting—our shortcomings. They have not only tried to create hostility toward us among specific nations, races, and religious groups. They have tried to prove our democracy an empty fraud, and our nation a consistent oppressor of underprivileged people. This may seem ludicrous to Americans, but it is sufficiently important to worry our friends.[39]

This is the most base example of pragmatism in the arena of civil rights for Southern blacks that one could possibly imagine. It sounds very principled and moral, but is really just a convoluted way of saying: "We've never stood for civil rights before. But if it helps us win friends and influence people in today's world, we're all for it!" As an example of the "new equality" in American society, Truman ordered the integration of the armed forces so black workers as well as whites could die to protect the capitalist system in Korea and later in Vietnam.

President Eisenhower continued the process of desegregating Southern society in order to make way for industrialization. His administration was responsible for passing the first Civil Rights Act (1957) and sending federal troops to Little Rock, Arkansas, to enforce the **desegregation** of the schools as required by the Supreme Court decision of 1954. He rationalized his actions in terms of international conditions for the expansion of the capitalist system as opposed to socialism.

In the South, as elsewhere, citizens are keenly aware of the tremendous disservice that has been done to the people of Arkansas in the eyes of the nation, and that has been done to the nation in the eyes of the world.

At a time when we face grave situations abroad because of the hatred that communism bears toward a system of government based on human rights, it would be difficult to exaggerate the harm that is being done to the prestige and influence, and indeed to the safety, of our nation and the world.

> Our enemies are gloating over this incident and using it everywhere to misrepresent our whole nation. We are portrayed as a violator of those standards of conduct which the people of the world united to proclaim in the Charter of the United Nations.[40]

As a follow-up, Eisenhower's administration implemented a second Civil Rights Act in 1960, the year John F. Kennedy was elected president.

About this time, the de-colonization of Africa was accelerating. The question of how to incline the new black nations of Africa toward a capitalist path of development (so bank capital could expand there) became a campaign issue. Kennedy understood that the reforming of Southern **social relations** remained the key to gearing up production for foreign markets, enhancing U.S. prestige in the world, and expanding U.S. control in the world.

> Today we are committed to a worldwide struggle to promote and protect the rights of all who wish to be free. And when Americans are sent to Vietnam or West Berlin we do not ask for whites only.
> We preach freedom around the world, and we mean it. And we cherish our freedom here at home. But are we to say to the world—and much more importantly to each other—that this is the land of the free, except for the Negroes; that we have no second-class citizens, except Negroes; that we have no class or caste system, no ghettos, no master race, except with respect to Negroes.[41]

Kennedy started the United States down the road to full-scale intervention in Vietnam, which Presidents Johnson and Nixon carried to its logical conclusion, laying waste to the whole of Indochina and sacrificing the mental and physical well-being of hundreds of thousands of young Americans impressed into the army, all in defense of "human rights."

The Johnson administration also understood the significance of the domestic issue of **civil rights** and implemented a third Civil Rights Act (1964) and the Voting Rights Act (1965). In his 1965 address to the graduating class of Howard University Johnson went so far as to equate the reform of Southern social relations with "revolution."

> Our earth is the home of revolution.
>
> In every corner of every continent men charged with hope contend with ancient ways in pursuit of justice. They reach for the newest of weapons to realize the oldest of dreams: that each may walk in freedom and pride, stretching his talents, enjoying the fruits of the earth.
>
> Our enemies may occasionally seize the day of change. But it is the banner of our revolution they take. And our own future is linked to this process of swift and turbulent change in many lands. But nothing, in any country, touches us more profoundly, nothing is more freighted with meaning for our own destiny, than the revolution of the Negro American.
>
> In far too many ways American Negroes have been another nation: deprived of freedom, crippled by hatred, the doors of opportunity closed to hope.
>
> In our time change has come to this nation too.[42]

In reality, the "revolution" is yet to come. So far, capitalist political leadership in this country has merely been confronted with a choice between a segregated Southern economy or one which could—in the words of former Governor Collins of Florida—meet "the challenge of accepting its part of the main stream of national life, and the responsibilities that go with it."[43]

> Advocates of racial and economic reaction—the very ones against whom we in the South have to struggle on a local and state level for every inch of progress we have made [should no longer] be allowed to speak for the South.[44]

It is this economic and social transformation which has laid the basis for real political revolution in the South and throughout the whole country in the current crisis. This also has international implications. The **general formula for political power** in this country has been that control of the Southern black (i.e., on the grounds of the color question and white supremacy) enables control of all Southern labor and the South, and that control of the Southern nation (i.e., the Solid South) enables control of Northern labor and the whole country. To this formulation we can also add a post-World War II appendix. Du Bois pointed out long ago that with the expansion of European imperialism into Asia and Africa the chief international "problem of the twentieth century [became] the problem of the color-line."[45] More particularly, since the rise to dominance of the United States in the world political-economy, the colonized status of the South has been the major international block to social change.

> Imperialism, the exploitation of colored labor throughout the world, thrives on the approval of the United States, and the United States gives that approval because of the South....
> The chief... and only obstacle to the coming of that kingdom of economic equality which is the only logical end of work is the determination of the white world to keep the black world poor and themselves rich. A clear vision of a world without inordinate individual wealth, of capital without profit and of income based on work alone, is the path out, not only for America but for all men. Across this path stands the South with flaming sword.[46]

Subsequent studies have amply documented the role of Dixiecrat Congressmen in the formulation of contemporary **foreign policy**.[47]

But just as the color question and the Solid South have been the main strength for capitalism and imperialism, "the oppression of the Negro people is the Achilles heel of United States imperialism."⁴⁸ To conform to the demands of the post-World War II era, the U.S. government has been compelled to reform economic, social, and political relations in the South. This means that the integration of the white and black workforces in the South is making the manipulation of the **color question** as the basis for controlling the South strategically more difficult. Today, "in order to attack the Negro workers, the government is going to have to attack and become entangled with the majority of the working class"⁴⁹ in the South.

Without the weapon of the color question there can be no **Solid South** and no divided working class under Democratic control. And without the solidly Democratic South there is no basis for Democratic co-optation of the Northern labor movement or Republican/Dixiecrat repression of labor.

Without control of the huge **labor movement**, it would prove less and less possible for the political representatives of capital in this country to command public support for the implementation of policies of economic aggrandizement and military intervention worldwide. This is the essence of the so-called breakdown in U.S. **foreign policy** today: the government has initiatives but cannot implement them because it lacks the wholehearted support of Northern labor; and it has not got the support of Northern labor because it has not got the same old Solid South with which to control labor.

New Implications for Northern Labor

This brings us back to the problem of labor's own political future. The conditions are clearly developing for a real **revolution** in labor's political role in the United States. The aging economy and the development of new technologies have led to another critical crisis for the country. The political representatives of different sections of capital are split and struggling over how to resolve the crisis and save the system. Organized labor in the North is on the ropes due to plant closings, unemployment, and membership loss. The old leadership which held the rank-and-file in the Democratic Party on the basis of the Solid South suddenly has nothing to offer. In the South the one-party system which controlled Southern labor through "divide-and-conquer" tactics—and which has been the lynchpin of the political system in the United States since its founding—is crumbling.

This last point is crucial. One prominent historian has concluded the following regarding the future of political life in the United States.

[O]ne fundamental development appears in a review of the past two decades: the emergence of a party system, which has opened the politics of the South to a range of possibility that would have seemed unthinkable just twenty years ago.[50]

So far this has been reflected in such developments as Republican presidential victories in the South and the decline of Democratic strength at state and local levels. In the long run, however, the Republicans can offer nothing to Southern labor except their traditional hard line against labor demands. Therefore the rejuvenation of a "Solid South" under the control of either major party seems improbable.[51]

Why is this not possible? First of all, because the Republican Party in the South represents the interests of Northern industries moved South. These Republicans have had visions of forging a new Solid South under their hegemony, but have found themselves in a bind. Goldwater tried to appeal to segregationist sentiment in 1964 and won some states, but the continual integration of the workforce has made this approach less effective over the years. Nixon and Reagan took more moderate approaches on the **color question** and did progressively better with Southern voters. The problem for them is that—as representatives of industrialists who are being hard pressed by this economic crisis—they have nothing they can promise or concede to workers in return for their electoral support.

The Democratic Party in the South faces some similar and

some different constraints. Like the Republicans, they too will ultimately find it impossible to rebuild the Solid South on the basis of the color line.

Indeed, the Democratic Party adopted a different tactic for controlling the Southern **black vote** by actually encouraging the development of the Southern Civil Rights Movement. Since the 1960s the mass of Southern blacks have voted the Democratic ticket more and more heavily in federal elections. A new group of **black leaders** also emerged who strengthened the ties between this block of voters and the Democrats. The power of this leadership was reinforced by the flow of **federal funds** into Southern social projects and economic maintenance programs needed especially by blacks. This leadership promised economic advance for all Southern blacks when in fact the only intention of the Democrats was to politically control the Negro People's Movement. With the current economic crisis and the drying up of federal programs in the South, the ability of this group of black leaders to politically contain the aspirations of the black masses is declining fast.

One Southern sociologist has emphasized the depth of the crisis in Southern black leadership.

> [O]ne has to recognize that the problems within the black community are often ones where the class difference between those who have made it and those who are still striving to make it have pretty much made many black leaders illegitimate in the eyes of the lower classes. If one looks at name recognition, for instance, among blacks, they recognize Jesse Jackson, they recognize other major figures, but they also recognize that many of those paths have not led to the kinds of progress that was promised. As a consequence, black leadership is often viewed as being bankrupt by those who are at the bottom. That's significant, and it's certainly not going to change in the very near future. . . .
>
> [T]here's a very real problem with the ability of black leaders to continue to perpetuate their status as leaders. In the Midwest one can find disillusionment with black leaders

like Jackson, Hatcher and others. In the Deep South that kind of process is going to unfold increasingly in the decades ahead. Promises have been made with no particular way that those promises are going to be kept. That kind of process is going to wreak havoc in internal dynamics in the black community in the years ahead.

What may begin to unfold is that those black leaders who claim to speak for blacks in the South are going to increasingly be recognized as having no connection with those blacks under those conditions. Blacks are not going to respond to the efforts on the part of leaders—or so-called leaders—to move in directions that are clearly not appropriate.[52]

Thus the objective basis exists for the breakout of Southern blacks from control by the Democratic Party. Their natural political allies are the white workers who today work elbow-to-elbow with them in plants across the South. On this basis the **class interests** of Southern workers could come to the fore and shatter Democratic control of the Southern labor movement on the traditional basis of the color line.

But the danger of the Democratic Party regaining control of Southern labor on the basis of the **color question** still exists. The one significant and alarming success of Southern Democrats in this regard occurred recently in Alabama. There the state AFL-CIO endorsed the erstwhile segregationist George Wallace for another term as governor. Contrary to national media reports, this did not represent acceptance of Wallace as a political leader by the majority of unskilled white and black laborers in the state. It was instead a reactionary position taken by the **skilled trades** of the state's small organized labor section. It was a replay of the more prosperous section of white farmers in the Populist movement going over to the side of Ben Tillman and the fascists in the Southern Democratic Party in the 1890s.

This has always been a tendency in Southern politics during critical crises. It is a dangerous tendency which threatens to split Southern labor along color lines. Such positions taken by

Southern AFL-CIO leaders must be opposed by AFL-CIO labor in the North with all its resources. The alternative is for Northern labor to once again fall sway to the coercion of the Solid South in the Democratic Party. AFL-CIO labor leaders who fail to combat this tendency are truly **misleaders** of the whole working class.

The only other prospect for continued control of the labor movement is the organization of a New Deal type coalition of white and black workers in the South. In fact, Jesse Jackson proposed such an alliance of integrated Southern labor with capital in his unprecedented speech before a joint session of the Alabama state legislature in May 1983. In the North that alignment was forged across the color line at the workplace. That would certainly be a possibility today in the South, except for one thing. The concession to Northern labor that won it to the Democratic Party was recognition of the **trade union movement**. That is the basis of the Democratic Party's strength in the basic industries of the North. A similar unionization concession in the South would necessitate governmental repeal of Section 14(b) of the Taft-Hartley Act. But that would undermine the whole reserve value of the separate national labor market and colonized economy of the South. Because this would adversely restrict the maneuvering room for finance capital in the future, the acceptability of this "solution" is doubtful.

In theory, the reform of Southern labor relations could be promoted as a stop-gap measure to prolong the life of the capitalist system. But it would mean the re-organization of the Democratic Party on a class basis: i.e., without the input of the fascist Southern industrialists. This could only lead to the increased clash of class interests in the political arena of the multinational state.

In the South, the old political system is unraveling rapidly. Here an intensified **class struggle** by Southern labor against the control of labor conditions by Northern capital and politicians—and against the complicity of Southern Democratic leaders in that control—is possible or even probable as the present critical crisis deepens.

As the South goes, so goes the North. The conditions exist for the coming undone of the Southern Democratic political machine.

Its ability to control congressional legislation to support and maintain the big city Democratic machines in the North is declining. In Chicago a harbinger of this was the successful Spring 1983 reform campaign by Harold Washington for mayor. At the end of that campaign the same Democratic leaders who earlier had opposed Washington—Kennedy and Mondale from the North and the six-member Bert Lance delegation from the South—were rushed into Chicago to voice support for and try to co-opt Washington into their camp. But the Washington campaign was the expression of an inevitable new trend toward independent political activity among Northern workers. Without the same old Solid South and because of the economic crisis, the Democratic Party can no more control this trend than it could maintain the graft and patronage-ridden Daley machine.

If ever there were a time which favored independent political activity by workers, this is it. If ever there were a time for speaking up and spelling out your interests, this is it. If ever the time were right for carrying the economic interests of the working population to their logical conclusion—**political power**—it is now.

Labor today has the opportunity to abolish forever its own exploitation at home and to establish permanent peace abroad. It is up to labor to develop the appropriate organizations and methods for accomplishing this and thus move the course of human history to its next stage of development: **jobs, peace and equality for all!**

APPENDIX A

BUSINESS RECESSIONS AND DEPRESSIONS IN THE UNITED STATES, 1796-PRESENT

Dates	Duration (months)
Experimental Party System	
1796-98	36
1802-03	24
1807-09	27
1815-21	71
Democratizing Party System	
1825-26	13
1833-34	9
1837-43	72
1857-58	18
Civil War Party System	
1866-67	18
1873-78	66
1882-85	36
1890-91	9
1893-97	48
Industrial Party System	
1907-08	12
1913-14	20
1920-21	18
1923-24	14
1926-27	13
1929-33	43
New Deal Party System	
1937-38	13
1948-49	11
1953-54	10
1957-58	8
1960-61	10
1969-70	11
1973-75	16
1980-present	

Sources: Morris, **Encyclopedia of American History**, 508-12; **Statistical Abstract of the United States, 1982-83**, Table 911.

APPENDIX B
CAPITAL TRENDS DATA SHEET
($ Billion)

Date	Value of Slaves	Capital Stock of Railroads	Book Value of Industries	Commercial Bank Assets
1850	2.0	0.3	0.5	0.5
1860	2.8	1.1	1.0	1.0
1870	0	2.5	1.7	1.8
1880		5.4	2.7	3.4
1890		9.0	5.7	6.4
1900		11.5	8.2	9.1
1910		18.4	16.9	19.3
1920		20.1	40.3	47.5
1930		22.8	59.1	64.1
1937		24.1	50.2	56.9
1948		18.2	113.6	149.8
1957		16.8	214.6	209.6
1967		14.7	218.0	415.4
1977		14.8	439.0	1176.6

Sources: Faulkner, **American Economic History**, 269, 548; **Historical Statistics of the United States, Colonial Times to 1970**, Series P-123, Q-347, Q-358, X-581, X-589; **Statistical Abstract of the United States, 1982-83**, Tables 826, 1088, 1377.

APPENDIX C
MAJOR WARS IN U.S. HISTORY, 1776-1973

Dates	Wars
Pre-Party Period	
1776-83	Revolutionary War
Experimental Party System	
1798-1800	War with France
1801-05	Tripolitan War
1812-14	War of 1812
1815	Algerian Intervention
1816-19	First Seminole War
Democratizing Party System	
1832	Black Hawk War
1835-43	Second Seminole War
1846-48	Mexican-American War
Civil War Party System	
1861-65	Civil War
1865-86	Apache/Sioux Wars
1890	Samoan Intervention
1893	Hawaiian Intervention
Industrial Party System	
1898	Spanish-American War
1899-1902	Cuban/Filipino Interventions
1900	Boxer Intervention
1903	Panamanian Intervention
1912-33	Nicaraguan Intervention
1913-17	Mexican Intervention
1915-34	Haitian Intervention
1917-18	World War I
1918-21	Soviet Intervention
New Deal Party System	
1941-45	World War II
1950-53	Korean War
1958	Lebanese Intervention
1965	Dominican Intervention
1964-73	Vietnam War

Source: Morris, **Encyclopedia of American History.**

APPENDIX D
TEXTILE SPINDLES IN THE SOUTH, 1880-1976

Year	Spindles (millions)	Percent of National Total	Percent of Cotton Consumed
1880	0.5	5.5	n.a.
1890	1.6	24.0	n.a.
1899	3.8	27.6	43
1914	13.0	35.5	50+
1921	16.1	43.5	n.a.
1930	18.6	59.5	78
1940	17.6	74.8	85
1950	17.7	81.1	91
1960	17.8	92.6	96
1970	18.7	97.9	98
1976	16.9	99.3	99

Sources: Faulkner, **American Economic History**, 565; Woodward, **Origins of the New South**, 132, 308; Vance, **Human Geography of the South**, 297; Morris, **Encyclopedia of American History**, 497-8; **Statistical Abstract of the United States, 1967, 1977.**

APPENDIX E
AVERAGE ANNUAL TEXTILE WAGES, 1921-1929

Region	U.S. Dollars				
	1921	1923	1925	1927	1929
New England	946	1010	961	1011	938
South	659	692	661	696	661
Difference	287	318	300	315	277
South as percent of New England	69.7	68.5	68.8	68.8	70.5

Source: Vance, **Human Geography of the South**, 294.

APPENDIX F
LUMBER PRODUCTION BY REGIONS, 1869-1919

	Percent of total					
Region	1869	1879	1889	1899	1909	1919
Northeast states	35.7	25.8	19.8	16.3	11.7	7.5
Great Lakes states	28.2	34.7	34.6	24.9	12.3	7.8
Southern states	10.1	13.8	20.3	31.7	44.9	46.6
Western states	4.9	4.5	9.6	9.9	18.4	29.3
Other states	21.2	21.2	15.7	17.2	12.7	8.9

Source: Faulkner, **American Economic History**, 565.

APPENDIX G
APPAREL INDUSTRY EMPLOYMENT BY REGION, 1950-1974

	Percent of total			
Region	1950	1960	1970	1974
Northeast	62.3	52.9	41.4	35.7
New York	33.9	25.8	18.3	14.9
South	16.7	27.9	39.8	44.2
North Carolina	1.1	2.9	5.5	6.1
Central	13.2	11.0	9.6	9.8
West	4.9	6.4	7.7	9.9

Source: **NACLA Report on the Americas**, March 1977, 11.

APPENDIX H
LEADING INDUSTRIES BY VALUE ADDED (1975)

	First	Second	Third
Northern regions			
Northeast	Machinery	Electrical equipment	Fabricated metal
Mid-Atlantic	Chemicals	Electrical equipment	Machinery
East North Central	Transport equipment	Machinery	Fabricated metal
West North Central	Food Processing	Machinery	Transport equipment
Southern regions			
South Atlantic	Textiles	Chemicals	Apparel
East South Central	Chemicals	Food processing	Machinery
West South Central	Chemicals	Electrical equipment	Food processing
Western regions			
Mountain	Food processing	Primary metals	Machinery
Pacific	Transport equipment	Food processing	Lumber

Source: **Statistical Abstract of the United States, 1977,** Table 1377.

APPENDIX I
PRIME MILITARY CONTRACTS BY REGION, 1939-1981

Percentage of total

Region	1939-45	1950-53	1960	1965	1970	1976	1981
Northeast	32.6	33.5	31.3	28.5	26.8	25.8	25.1
Midwest	38.0	34.6	18.4	19.0	19.5	13.3	17.2
South	16.0	13.3	18.5	23.7	29.2	24.9	30.7
West	13.4	18.6	31.8	28.8	24.5	31.0	27.1

Sources: Keller, "The Militarization of the Southern Economy," 39; **Statistical Abstract of the United States, 1982-83**, Table 582.

APPENDIX J
THIRD PARTY SEATS IN CONGRESS, 1789-1976

Years	House	Senate	Total	Relevant Events
1789-1828	0	0	0	End of Experimental System
1830-32	37	5	42	**Early Democratizing Realignment**
1834	0	0	0	Realignment complete
1836-40	10	3	13	Intermediate crisis
1842	1	1	2	End of crisis
1854-60	33	6	39	**Early Civil War Realignment**
1864	0	0	0	Realignment complete
1870-74	11	4	15	Intermediate crisis
1876	0	1	1	End of crisis
1878-82	12	1	13	Intermediate crisis
1884	2	0	2	End of crisis
1890-92	10	2	12	Intermediate crisis
1894-96	24	6	30	**Early Industrial Realignment**
1902	0	0	0	Realignment complete
1912-14	12	1	13	Intermediate crisis
1920	1	0	1	End of crisis
1922	5	2	7	Intermediate crisis
1928	1	1	2	End of crisis
1934-36	11	3	14	**Early New Deal Realignment**
1938-40	4	3	7	Intermediate crisis
1946	1	0	1	Realignment complete
1972-74	1	2	3	Intermediate crisis
1976	0	1	1	End of crisis

Sources: **Historical Statistics of the United States, Colonial Times to 1970,** Series Y-206, 290; **Statistical Abstract of the United States,** 1982-83, Table 788.

References

CHAPTER 1

1. "The General Council to the Federal Council of Romance Switzerland." In: **Minutes, The General Council of the First International, 1868-1870**. Quoted in: Karl Marx and Frederick Engels, **Selected Works**, Vol. 2 (Moscow, 1973), 174-75.
2. Ibid., 175-76.
3. Ibid., 176.
4. Ibid.
5. Ibid., 176-77.
6. Ludwell Denny, **America Conquers Britain** (New York, 1930), 407. Quoted in: R. Palme Dutt, **World Politics, 1918-1936** (New York, 1936), 347.
7. **New York Herald Tribune**, 29 December 1930. Quoted in: Harold R. Bruce, **American Parties and Politics** (New York, 1936), 58.
8. Noam Chomsky and Edward S. Herman, **The Washington Connection and Third World Fascism** (Boston, 1979).
9. Karl Marx, **Capital**, Vol. 1 (New York, 1967), 301.

CHAPTER 2

1. Paul Binding, **Separate Country: A Literary Journey Through**

178 REFERENCES

the American South (London, 1979), 32-34.
   2. Andre Gunder Frank, **Dependent Accumulation and Underdevelopment** (New York, 1979), 81-85.
   3. Clement Eaton, **A History of the Old South** (New York, 1966), 373-74.
   4. Ibid., 374.
   5. Ibid., 374-76.
   6. Karl Marx, **Capital**, Vol. 1 (New York, 1967), 747-49.
   7. **Die Presse**, 7 November 1861. In: Karl Marx and Frederick Engels, **The Civil War in the United States** (New York, 1971), 72-73.
   8. **Die Presse**, 25 October 1861. In: Marx and Engels, **Civil War in the U.S.**, 66-68.
   9. Ibid., 69.
   10. Ibid., 64.
   11. Ibid., 68-69.
   12. Ibid., 64.
   13. Leonard Dinnerstein, Roger L. Nichols, and David M. Reimers, **Natives and Strangers: Ethnic Groups and the Building of America** (New York, 1979), 60.
   14. **Die Presse**, 7 November 1861. In: Marx and Engels, **Civil War in the U.S.**, 79-81.
   15. Louis M. Hacker, **The Triumph of American Capitalism** (New York, 1947), 340.
   16. Ibid., 344.
   17. Rupert B. Vance, **Human Geography of the South** (Chapel Hill, 1932), 470.
   18. C. Vann Woodward, **Origins of the New South, 1877-1913** (Baton Rouge, 1951), 179.
   19. Ibid., 291-92.
   20. George B. Tindall, **The Emergence of the New South, 1913-1945** (Baton Rouge, 1967), 462.
   21. Woodward, **Origins of the New South**, 306-307.
   22. Tindall, **Emergence of the New South**, 443-44.
   23. Philip S. Foner, **Organized Labor and the Black Worker, 1619-1973** (New York, 1976), 277-81.
   24. Fred A. Hartley, Jr., **Our New National Labor Policy** (New York, 1948), 150-51.
   25. General Baker, Jr., **Repeal Section 14(b) of the Taft-Hartley Act** (Chicago, 1977), 9, 12-13.
   26. Ibid., 5.
   27. Willie Baptist, "A Critique of the Communist Party USA's 'Struggle for Afro-American Liberation'," **Appeal to Reason** 6 (Summer 1980): 17.

CHAPTER 3

1. J. G. Randall and David Donald, **The Civil War and Reconstruction** (Lexington, Mass., 1969), 419-20.
2. W. E. B. Du Bois, **Black Reconstruction in America** (New York, 1935), chapter 4.
3. C. Vann Woodward, **Reunion and Reaction** (Boston, 1951), 147.
4. Frederick Engels, **Socialism: Utopian and Scientific** (New York, 1972), 63-64.
5. Karl Marx, **Capital**, Afterword to the Second Edition (New York, 1967), 14.
6. Karl Marx, **The Poverty of Philosophy** (New York, 1967), 111.
7. S. Menshikov, **The Economic Cycle: Postwar Developments** (Moscow, 1975), 190.
8. Craig S. Volland, "The Passing of the Hydrocarbon Era," **High Technology** (January 1983): 74.
9. "Can There Be Detente the Second Time Around?" **Rally, Comrades!** 1 (May 1981): 2.
10. Harold U. Faulkner, **American Economic History** (New York, 1929), 242-60.
11. Richard B. Morris, **Encyclopedia of American History**. (New York, 1953), 506.
12. Jeff Frieden, "Borrowing from Commercial Banks by the Less Developed Countries," **Appeal to Reason** 6 (Summer 1980): 57-78.
13. Numan V. Bartley and Hugh D. Graham, **Southern Politics and the Second Reconstruction** (Baltimore, 1976), 1-2.
14. Ibid., 3.
15. Ibid.
16. Ibid., 4.
17. C. Vann Woodward, **Origins of the New South, 1877-1913** (Baton Rouge, 1951), 312-14.
18. Bartley and Graham, **Southern Politics**, 5.
19. Ibid., 7.
20. Ibid., 13.
21. "Can There Be Detente the Second Time Around?" **Rally, Comrades!** 1 (May 1981): 2.
22. "The Path to Power and the Role of the Party," **Rally, Comrades!** 2 (May 1982): 1.
23. Nelson A. Rockefeller, **The Rockefeller Report on the Americas** (Chicago, 1969), 102-103.
24. John Naisbitt, **Megatrends: Ten New Directions Transforming Our Lives** (New York, 1982), 59-66.

25. "Chip Wars," **Business Week**, 23 May 1983, 81.
26. Morris, **Encyclopedia of American History**, 508.
27. Louis M. Hacker, **The Triumph of American Capitalism** (New York, 1947), 178.
28. Morris, **Encyclopedia of American History**, 509.
29. Hacker, **Triumph of American Capitalism**, 213.
30. Morris, **Encyclopedia of American History**, 509.
31. Hacker, **Triumph of American Capitalism**, 214.
32. James B. Walker, **The Epic of American Industry** (New York, 1949), 139.
33. Faulkner, **American Economic History**, 499-500.
34. Hacker, **Triumph of American Capitalism**, 404.
35. Arthur C. Bining and Thomas C. Cochran, **The Rise of American Economic Life** (New York, 1964), 413.
36. Faulkner, **American Economic History**, 635.
37. Ibid., 636-37.
38. Bining and Cochran, **Rise of American Economic Life**, 419.
39. Ibid., 519.
40. Ibid., 638.
41. Morris, **Encyclopedia of American History**, 511.
42. Ibid., 511-12.
43. A. Leontiev, **Political Economy** (New York, n.d.), 237.
44. Menshikov, **The Economic Cycle**, 102.
45. Herbert M. Morais, **The Struggle for American Freedom** (New York, 1944), 100-101.
46. Morris, **Encyclopedia of American History**, 495.
47. Ibid., 497.
48. Woodward, **Origins of the New South**, 120-22.
49. Ibid., 123-24.
50. Franklin D. Roosevelt, Foreword to the National Emergency Council's **Report on Economic Conditions of the South** (Washington, D.C., 1938), 1.
51. Calvin B. Hoover and B. U. Ratchford, **Economic Resources and Policies of the South** (New York, 1951), 155-56.
52. Ibid., 162.
53. General Baker, Jr., **The UAW Faces the 80's** (Chicago, n.d.), 4-10.
54. Hoover and Ratchford, **Economic Resources**, 156.
55. Kirkpatrick Sale, **Power Shift: The Rise of the Southern Rim and Its Challenge to the Eastern Establishment** (New York, 1976).
56. Hoover and Ratchford, **Economic Resources**, 160-61.
57. "Bourgeois Policy Struggles of the '80s," **Rally, Comrades!** 2 (July 1982): 2.

58. Hoover and Ratchford, **Economic Resources**, 161.
59. **Statistical Abstract of the United States, 1982-83** (Washington, D.C., 1982), Table 1381.
60. "Electronics: The Global Industry," **NACLA** (April 1977): 10.
61. John F. Keller, "The Militarization of the Southern Economy," **Appeal to Reason** 6 (Summer 1980): 43-44.
62. Naisbitt, **Megatrends**, 210-214.

CHAPTER 4

1. "Bourgeois Policy Struggles of the '80s," **Rally, Comrades!** 2 (July 1982): 4.
2. Ibid.
3. "Can There Be Detente the Second Time Around?" **Rally, Comrades!** 1 (May 1981): 2.
4. Karl Marx and Frederick Engels, **Selected Works**, Vol. 1 (Moscow, 1973), 116.
5. William Serrin, "Union Membership Falls Sharply; Decline Expected to be Permanent," **The New York Times**, 31 May 1983, 6.
6. Nelson Peery, **The Negro National Colonial Question** (Chicago, 1975), 97.
7. **New York Daily Tribune**, 11 October 1861. In: Karl Marx and Frederick Engels, **The Civil War in the United States** (New York, 1971), 6.
8. **New York Herald Tribune**, 29 December 1930. Quoted in: Harold R. Bruce, **American Parties and Politics** (New York, 1936), 58.
9. Ibid.
10. Ibid.
11. Ibid.
12. W. E. B. Du Bois, **Black Reconstruction in America** (New York, 1935), 240, 706.
13. Peery, **Negro National Colonial Question**, 99.
14. "Tito and Modern Revisionism," **People's Tribune**, 12 August 1980, 1.
15. Clement Eaton, **A History of the Old South** (New York, 1966), 153.
16. Lee Norton, **War Elections, 1862-1864** (New York, 1944), 18-20.
17. Du Bois, **Black Reconstruction**, 291.
18. Ibid., 596.
19. Frank Freidel, **F.D.R. and the South** (Baton Rouge, 1965), 1-2.
20. George B. Tindall, **The Disruption of the Solid South** (New

York, 1972), 29.
21. Freidel, **F.D.R. and the South**, 86.
22. Ibid., 48.
23. V. O. Key, **Southern Politics in State and Nation** (New York, 1949), 355.
24. Fred A. Hartley, Jr., **Our New National Labor Policy** (New York, 1948), 26.
25. Ibid., 26-27.
26. Ibid., 74.
27. Tindall, **Disruption of the Solid South**, 42.
28. See, for example, Reg Murphy and Hal Gulliver, **The Southern Strategy** (New York, 1971).
29. Michael Harrington, **Decade of Decision: The Crisis of the American System** (New York, 1980), 310.

CHAPTER 5

1. "Is the South Changing?" Transcript of **Firing Line**, Series No. 533 (Columbia, S.C., 1982), 9-10.
2. Ibid., 8-9.
3. Karl Marx, **Capital**, Vol. 1 (New York, 1967), 301.
4. W. E. B. Du Bois, **Black Reconstruction in America** (New York, 1935), 377.
5. W. E. B. Du Bois, **An ABC of Color** (New York, 1971), 110.
6. Karl Marx and Frederick Engels, **The German Ideology** (New York, 1981), 65-66.
7. "Color Question—Aspect of National Question," **Rally, Comrades!** 1 (August 1981): 2.
8. Ibid.
9. George V. Plekhanov, **Fundamental Problems of Marxism** (New York, 1969), 97.
10. Herbert Aptheker, **Essays in the History of the American Negro** (New York, 1945).
11. Richard B. Morris, **Encyclopedia of American History** (New York, 1953), 514.
12. Ibid., 175-76.
13. Clement Eaton, **A History of the Old South** (New York, 1966), 353.
14. Ibid., 356.
15. Du Bois, **Black Reconstruction**, 185.
16. Ibid., 347, 352-53.
17. William Z. Foster, **The Negro People in American History** (New York, 1970), 376-86.

18. W. J. Cash, **The Mind of the South** (New York, 1970), 159-60.
19. Lewis H. Blair, **A Southern Prophesy: The Prosperity of the South Dependent Upon the Elevation of the Negro** (Boston, 1964), 25-28.
20. Cash, **The Mind of the South**, 158-59, 161.
21. C. Vann Woodward, **The Strange Career of Jim Crow** (New York, 1957), 67-68, 81-83.
22. Congressional Record, 69th Congress, 2nd Session, p. 5362. Quoted in: George B. Tindall, **The Disruption of the Solid South** (New York, 1972), 47.
23. Woodward, **The Strange Career of Jim Crow**, 83.
24. Sue Thrasher and Leah Wise, "The Southern Tenant Farmers' Union," **Southern Exposure** 1 (Winter 1974): 6.
25. Katharine DuPre Lumpkin, **The South in Progress** (New York, 1940), 137-59; Philip S. Foner, **Organized Labor and the Black Worker, 1619-1973** (New York, 1976), 238-68.
26. Lumpkin, **The South in Progress**, 93-116; Robert L. Zangrando, "The NAACP and a Federal Anti-Lynching Bill." In: Bernard Sternsher (ed.), **The Negro in Depression and War** (Chicago, 1969), 181-92.
27. James S. Allen, **The Negro Question in the United States** (New York, 1936), 94-115; Harry Haywood, **Negro Liberation** (New York, 1948), 49-65.
28. Lumpkin, **The South in Progress**, 160-85; John A. Salmond, "The Civilian Conservation Corps and the Negro." In: Sternsher, **The Negro in Depression and War**, 78-92.
29. Haywood, **Negro Liberation**, 80-81.
30. Bill Finger and Mike Krivosh, "Stevens vs. Justice," **Southern Exposure** 4 (Spring/Summer 1976): 38-44; Carolyn Ashbaugh and Dan McCurry, "On the Line at Oneita," ibid., 30-37.
31. Liz Wheaton, "The Third of November," **Southern Exposure** 9 (Fall 1981): 55-67.
32. Laughlin McDonald, "Voting Rights on the Chopping Block," **Southern Exposure** 9 (Spring 1981): 89-94; Judy Hand and Scott Douglas, "Enough is Enough," ibid., 95-98.
33. "Color Question—Aspect of National Question," **Rally, Comrades!** 1 (August 1981): 2.
34. Nelson Peery, **The Negro National Colonial Question** (Chicago, 1975), 55-56.
35. President's Committee on Civil Rights, **To Secure These Rights** (Washington, D.C., 1947). In: Albert P. Blaustein and Robert L. Zangrando (eds.), **Civil Rights and the American Negro** (New York, 1968), 377-78.
36. Victor Perlo, **The Negro in Southern Agriculture** (New York,

1953), 110-11.
37. John F. Keller, "The Militarization of the Southern Economy," **Appeal to Reason** 6 (Summer 1980): 37.
38. Peery, **The Negro National Colonial Question**, 56.
39. President's Committee, **To Secure These Rights**. In: Blaustein and Zangrando (eds.), **Civil Rights and the American Negro**, 378-79.
40. Dwight D. Eisenhower, **The New York Times**, 25 September 1957. In: Ibid., 457.
41. John F. Kennedy, **The New York Times**, 12 June 1963. In: Ibid., 484, 486.
42. Lyndon B. Johnson, White House Press Release, 4 June 1965. In: Ibid., 559.
43. LeRoy Collins, Speech at Princeton University, 1960. Quoted in: Monroe Lee Billington, **The Political South in the Twentieth Century** (New York, 1975), 124.
44. Ibid., 124-25.
45. Du Bois, **An ABC of Color**, 20.
46. Du Bois, **Black Reconstruction**, 706-707.
47. Charles O. Lerche, **The Uncertain South: Its Changing Patterns of Politics in Foreign Policy** (Chicago, 1964).
48. Victor Perlo, **American Imperialism** (New York, 1951), 91.
49. Peery, **The Negro National Colonial Question**, 56.
50. Tindall, **Disruption of the Solid South**, 72.
51. Ibid., 60-71.
52. "Is the South Changing?" Transcript of **Firing Line**, 3.

Bibliography

BOOKS

Allen, James S. **The Negro Question in the United States.** New York: International, 1936.

Aptheker, Herbert. **Essays in the History of the American Negro.** New York: International, 1945.

Bartley, Numan V., and Hugh D. Graham. **Southern Politics and the Second Reconstruction.** Baltimore: Johns Hopkins Univ. Press, 1976.

Billington, Monroe Lee. **The Political South in the Twentieth Century.** New York: Scribners, 1975.

Binding, Paul. **Separate Country: A Literary Journey Through the American South.** London: Paddington, 1979.

Bining, Arthur C., and Thomas C. Cochran. **The Rise of American Economic Life.** New York: Scribners, 1964.

Blair, Lewis H. **A Southern Prophesy: The Prosperity of the South Dependent Upon the Elevation of the Negro.** Boston: Little, Brown, 1964.

Blaustein, Albert P., and Robert L. Zangrando, eds. **Civil Rights and the American Negro.** New York: Washington Square, 1968.

Bruce, Harold R. **American Parties and Politics.** New York: Holt, 1936.

Cash, W. J. **The Mind of the South.** New York: Knopf, 1970.

Chomsky, Noam, and Edward S. Herman. **The Washington Connection and Third World Fascism.** Boston: South End, 1979.

Coulter, E. Merton. **The Confederate States of America.** Baton Rouge: Louisiana State Univ. Press, 1950.

Craven, Avery O. **The Growth of Southern Nationalism, 1848-1861**. Baton Rouge: Louisiana State Univ. Press, 1953.

Dinnerstein, Leonard, Roger L. Nichols, and David M. Reimers. **Natives and Strangers: Ethnic Groups and the Building of America**. New York: Oxford Univ. Press, 1979.

Du Bois, W. E. B. **An ABC of Color**. New York: International, 1971.

———. **Black Reconstruction in America**. New York: Russell, 1935.

Dutt, R. Palme. **World Politics, 1918-1936**. New York: International, 1936.

Eaton, Clement. **A History of the Old South**. New York: Macmillan, 1966.

Engels, Frederick. **Socialism: Utopian and Scientific**. New York: International, 1972.

Faulkner, Harold U. **American Economic History**. New York: Harpers, 1929.

Foner, Philip S. **Organized Labor and the Black Worker, 1619-1973**. New York: International, 1976.

Foster, William Z. **The Negro People in American History**. New York: International, 1970.

Frank, Andre Gunder. **Dependent Accumulation and Underdevelopment**. New York: Monthly Review, 1979.

Freidel, Frank. **F.D.R. and the South**. Baton Rouge: Louisiana State Univ. Press, 1965.

Hacker, Louis M. **The Triumph of American Capitalism**. New York: Columbia Univ. Press, 1947.

Harrington, Michael. **Decade of Decision: The Crisis of the American System**. New York: Simon and Schuster, 1980.

Hartley, Fred A., Jr. **Our New National Labor Policy**. New York: Funk and Wagnalls, 1948.

Haywood, Harry. **Negro Liberation**. New York: International, 1948.

Hoover, Calvin B., and B. U. Ratchford. **Economic Resources and Policies of the South**. New York: Macmillan, 1951.

Key, V. O. **Southern Politics in State and Nation**. New York: Vintage, 1949.

Leontiev, A. **Political Economy**. New York: International, n.d.

Lerche, Charles O. **The Uncertain South: Its Changing Patterns of Politics in Foreign Policy**. Chicago: Quadrangle, 1964.

Lumpkin, Katharine DuPre. **The South in Progress**. New York: International, 1940.

McCardell, John. **The Idea of a Southern Nation: Southern Nationalists and Southern Nationalism, 1830-1860**. New York: Norton, 1979.

Marx, Karl. **Capital**. Vol. 1. New York: International, 1967.

———. **The Poverty of Philosophy.** New York: International, 1967.
Marx, Karl, and Frederick Engels. **The Civil War in the United States.** New York: International, 1971.
———. **The German Ideology.** New York: International, 1981.
———. **Selected Works.** Vols. 1-2. Moscow: Progress, 1973.
Menshikov, S. **The Economic Cycle: Postwar Developments.** Moscow: Progress, 1975.
Morais, Herbert M. **The Struggle for American Freedom.** New York: International, 1944.
Morris, Richard B. **Encyclopedia of American History.** New York: Harper Brothers, 1953.
Murphy, Reg, and Hal Gulliver. **The Southern Strategy.** New York: Scribners, 1971.
Naisbitt, John. **Megatrends: Ten New Directions Transforming Our Lives.** New York: Warner Books, 1982.
Norton, Lee. **War Elections, 1862-1864.** New York: International, 1944.
Odum, Howard W. **Southern Regions of the United States.** Chapel Hill: Univ. of North Carolina Press, 1936.
Peery, Nelson. **The Negro National Colonial Question.** Chicago: Workers Press, 1975.
Perlo, Victor. **American Imperialism.** New York: International, 1951.
———. **The Negro in Southern Agriculture.** New York: International, 1953.
Plekhanov, George V. **Fundamental Problems of Marxism.** New York: International, 1969.
Randall, J. G., and David Donald. **The Civil War and Reconstruction.** Lexington, Mass.: Heath, 1969.
Rockefeller, Nelson A. **The Rockefeller Report on the Americas.** Chicago: Quadrangle, 1969.
Roosevelt, Franklin D. Foreword to the National Emergency Council's **Report on Economic Conditions of the South.** Washington, D.C.: Government Printing Office, 1938.
Sale, Kirkpatrick. **Power Shift: The Rise of the Southern Rim and Its Challenge to the Eastern Establishment.** New York: Vintage, 1976.
Sternsher, Bernard, ed. **The Negro in Depression and War.** Chicago: Quadrangle, 1969.
Tindall, George B. **The Emergence of the New South, 1913-1945.** Baton Rouge: Louisiana State Univ. Press, 1967.
———. **The Disruption of the Solid South.** New York: Norton, 1972.
Vance, Rupert B. **Human Geography of the South.** Chapel Hill:

Univ. of North Carolina Press, 1932.

Van Sickle, John V. **Planning for the South: An Inquiry into the Economics of Regionalism**. Nashville: Vanderbilt Univ. Press, 1943.

Walker, James B. **The Epic of American Industry**. New York: Harper, 1949.

Woodward, C. Vann. **Origins of the New South, 1877-1913**. Baton Rouge: Louisiana State Univ. Press, 1951.

———. **Reunion and Reaction**. Boston: Little, Brown, 1951.

———. **The Strange Career of Jim Crow**. New York: Oxford Univ. Press, 1957.

PAMPHLETS

Baker, General, Jr. **Repeal Section 14(b) of the Taft-Hartley Act**. Chicago: Workers Press, 1977.

———. **The UAW Faces the 80's**. Chicago: Workers Press, n.d.

ARTICLES

Ashbaugh, Carolyn, and Dan McCurry. "On the Line at Oneita." **Southern Exposure** 4 (Spring/Summer 1976): 30-37.

Baptist, Willie. "A Critique of the Communist Party USA's 'Struggle for Afro-American Liberation'." **Appeal to Reason** 6 (Summer 1980): 9-20.

Finger, Bill, and Mike Krivosh. "Stevens vs. Justice." **Southern Exposure** 4 (Spring/Summer 1976): 38-44.

Frieden, Jeff. "Borrowing from Commercial Banks by the Less Developed Countries: Past, Present and Future." **Appeal to Reason** 6 (Summer 1980): 57-78.

Hand, Judy, and Scott Douglas. "Enough is Enough." **Southern Exposure** 9 (Spring 1981): 95-98.

Keller, John F. "The Militarization of the Southern Economy." **Appeal to Reason** 6 (Summer 1980): 31-47.

McDonald, Laughlin. "Voting Rights on the Chopping Block." **Southern Exposure** 9 (Spring 1981): 89-94.

Volland, Craig S. "The Passing of the Hydrocarbon Era." **High Technology** (January 1983).

Wheaton, Liz. "The Third of November." **Southern Exposure** 9 (Fall 1981): 55-67.

OTHER PERIODICALS

Business Week, 23 May 1983, 80-96.

NACLA Report on the Americas, March 1977.
——, April 1977.
People's Tribune 12 August 1980, 1-2.
Rally, Comrades! 1 (May 1981): 1-2.
—— 1 (August 1981): 2.
—— 2 (May 1982): 1.
—— 2 (July 1982): 2.

GOVERNMENT PUBLICATIONS

Historical Statistics of the United States, Colonial Times to 1970. Washington, D.C.: Government Printing Office, 1975.
Statistical Abstract of the United States. Washington, D.C.: Government Printing Office, 1914-1982.

TRANSCRIPTS

Firing Line. Series No. 533. Columbia, S.C.: Southern Educational Communications Association, 1982.

Name Index

Adams, John, 121
Agnew, Spiro, 131

Barden, Graham, 129
Binding, Paul, 15
Blair, Lewis H., 149-50
Buchanan, James, 33, 38, 39
Buckley, William F., 135
Burr, Aaron, 34, 121
Bush, George, 131
Byrd, Harry, 129

Carter, Jimmy, 131
Clay, Henry, 124
Clinton, George, 121
Cobb, James C., 135
Collins, LeRoy, 161
Cooke, Jay, 77
Coolidge, Calvin, 13, 116, 151
Coulter, E. Merton, 31
Craven, Avery O., 31

Deere, John, 24
Dowd, Douglas, 19
Du Bois, W. E. B., 114, 116, 123, 136, 162

Eads, James B., 53
Eastland, James, 114
Eisenhower, Dwight D., 92-93, 132, 159-60

Faulkner, William, 143
Fisher, O. C., 129
Flournoy, John Jacobus, 145
Frank, Andre Gunder, 19-20

Godkin, Edwin L., 46
Goldwater, Barry, 164
Grant, Ulysses S., 51-52
Gregg, William, 25-27

Harrington, Michael, 132-33
Hartley, Fred J., 47, 128-29
Hatcher, Richard, 166
Hayes, Rutherford B., 124, 126
Helper, Hinton Rowan, 144-45
Hoover, Calvin B., 89
Huger, Alfred, 144
Humphrey, Hubert H., 130

NAME INDEX

Jackson, Jesse, 165-67
Jefferson, Thomas, 33, 119, 121
Johnson, Lyndon B., 96, 130, 157, 160-61

Kendall, Postmaster General, 144
Kennedy, Edward M., 168
Kennedy, John F., 130, 157, 160
Key, V. O., 128
Kondratieff, Nicolai D., 56

Lance, Bert, 168
Lee, Robert E., 52
Lincoln, Abraham, 39, 124
Lucas, Wingate, 129

McCardell, John, 31
McDuffie, Governor, 144
Madison, James, 121
Marshall, George, 93
Marshall, John, 34
Marx, Karl, 57, 118
Michener, James A., 130
Millner, Steven, 135
Mondale, Walter, 131, 168
Moorehead, F. C., 44

Napoleon, 33
Nixon, Richard M., 70, 131-32, 160, 164

Odum, Howard W., 89

Palmer, A. Mitchell, 109
Pierce, Franklin, 38
Polk, James, 38
Pratt, David, 24
Price, Reynolds, 15

Ratchford, B. U., 89
Reagan, Ronald, 118, 131, 164
Rockefeller, Nelson, 70, 93
Roosevelt, Franklin D., 89, 96, 127-28, 158

Sale, Kirkpatrick, 91, 96
Stevens, Thaddeus, 12

Taft, Robert, 47
Tilden, Samuel J., 124, 126
Tillman, Ben, 151, 166
Tindall, George B., 15
Toombs, Senator, 31
Truman, Harry, 156, 158

Vance, Rupert B., 15, 89
Van Sickle, John V., 89

Wallace, George, 166
Washington, Harold, 168
Whitney, Eli, 24
Williams, Tennessee, 143
Winpisinger, William, 132
Wood, John, 129
Woodward, C. Vann, 15, 124, 140

Subject Index

Banks
  Credit Mobilier, 76
  financiers, 133
  International Monetary
    Fund, 82
  Jay Cooke and Company, 77
  Mellons, 44
  Morgan Guaranty Trust, 44,
    81, 87
  National City Bank, 78-79
  relation to manufacturing, 62
  Rockefellers, 44
  Wall Street, 71
  World Bank, 82
Black Reconstruction in
  America (Du Bois), 114
Business Week, 71

Canada, 9, 13, 18
Capital, 5
  crises, 100-107
  financial section, 155
  historical sectors, 58, 170
  investments, 59
  political splits, 101-103
  relation to state, 107
Capitalism, 2-6
  collectivized production, 3
  machine basis, 54
  private ownership, 3
  reform of, 111
  rise of nations, 5
  slavery basis, 54
  social basis of production, 56
Charleston Courier, 27
Charleston News and
  Courier, 153
Civil War, 10-12, 21, 40-41, 59, 62
  Battle of the Wilderness, 51
  economic legislation, 42
  general strike by slaves, 52
Colonies
  Hat Act, 23
  Iron Act, 23
  Navigation Acts, 23
  North American, 21-23
  putting-out system, 24
  Woolens Act, 23
Colonization of South: see
  Southern colonization
Color question, 14, 135-68
  Abolitionists, 42, 100
  American Nazi Party, 154
  basis of Solid South, 137-39
  black vote, 138
  Carpetbaggers, 100
  color line, 137
  control of labor, 142-54
  fascism, 153
  Freedom Riders, 100

Color question, *continued*
  KKK, 143, 154
  moral issue, 100, 137
  poor whites, 10, 143
  social reform, 100
  two-party system, 155
  white supremacy, 154
  white workers, 138
Confederate States of America
  (Coulter), 31
Confederation, 21-23
  Articles of Confederation, 21, 22
  central state, 23
  class interests, 23
  Committees of Safety, 21
  Continental Congress, 21
  land claims, 22
  provincial congresses, 21
  Public Domain, 22
  Treaty of Paris (1783), 23
Cotton
  gin, 24
  National Cotton Planters' Association, 44
  production, 25, 26, 85
Crises, 72-83, 169
  Black Friday, 76
  intermediate, 72
  land speculation, 24, 74-75, 81
  monetary, 82
  railroad speculation, 75-78
  rate of profit, 83
  realignment cycle, 72-83
  relation to wars, 72-83
  stock speculation, 80-81
  trade speculation, 74-75
Crises for labor
  job dislocations, 97
  poverty, 102
  unemployment, 97, 102
  wage cuts, 108
Critical crises, 55, 63, 100
  1784-1788, 73
  1815-1821, 74
  1857-1858, 75
  1893-1897, 63, 77, 148, 150
  1929-1933, 63, 152
  1980-present, 63, 83
Democratic Party: *see*
  Two-party systems
Desegregation: economics
  decolonization process, 155
  European reconstruction, 155
  finance capital, 155
  integration, 158
  mechanization of cotton, 156
  militarization of economy, 155
  Negro people's movement, 157-58
  proletarianization, 157
  segregation laws, 157
Desegregation: impact on capital
  color question, 163
  foreign policy, 163
  labor movement, 163
  Solid South, 163
Desegregation: impact on labor, 163-68
  black leaders, 165
  black vote, 165
  class interests, 166
  class struggle, 167
  color question, 164, 166
  federal funds, 165
  misleaders, 167
  political power, 168
  revolution, 163
  skilled trades, 166
  trade union movement, 167
Desegregation: politics, 158-63
  civil rights, 161
  Civil Rights Act (1957), 159
  Civil Rights Act (1960), 160
  Civil Rights Act (1964), 161
  decolonization, 160
  foreign policy, 162
  social reform, 158
  social relations, 160
  Supreme Court, 159
  Voting Rights Act (1965), 161

Economic periods, 58, 62

banking industry, 59
carrying trade, 57
cotton industry, 59
manufacturing, 59
railroad industry, 59
Economic programs, 72
    Agricultural Adjustment Act
       (1933), 153
    Atari Democrats, 71
    Civil War, 42
    Council on Foreign Relations,
       93, 102
    Hamiltonian, 42
    hemispheric division of labor,
       70-71, 107
    Jacksonian, 42
    Keynesian, 82
    militarization of economy, 82
    National Recovery Act, 47
    New Deal, 42
    New Right, 70
    Pentagon, 94
    Reaganomics, 42, 132
    reindustrialization, 70, 101-102
    supply-side economics, 101-102
    Taft-Hartley Act (1947), 47-48,
       110, 128-29
    Trilateralists, 102
    wage-price freeze, 132
Economic realignments, 56,
    57-63
    business cycle, 55, 169
    capital investments, 58
    crises of overproduction, 54
    structure of economy, 55
Economic reserve, 142
Economic Resources and
    Policies of the South
    (Hoover and
    Ratchford), 89
Elections
    1856, 38
    1860, 39
    1862, 122
    1876, 124
Emergence of the New South
    (Tindall), 15

England, 6-11
    Acts of Union (1707, 1800), 6
    Irish question, 7-10
Essays on Domestic Industry
    (Gregg), 27

Factors in Southern
    nationalism, 140-42
    Negro people's movement,
       142-43
    political, 141
    poor whites, 143
    white workers, 138
Firing Line television show, 135
Formula for political power, 1,
    114, 134, 138, 162
    class interests, 14
    conscious use, 116
    electoral politics, 117
    foreign policy, 162
    ideologies, 115
    labor vote, 100
    Southern question, 118
    state power, 115
    third parties, 114
    United Kingdom, 5-11, 118
    United States, 12-14, 114-18

Growth of Southern
    Nationalism
    (Craven), 31

High Technology, 56
Human Geography of the South
    (Vance), 15

Idea of a Southern Nation
    (McCardell), 31
Impending Crisis of the South
    (Helper), 144
Imperialist methods
    export of finance capital,
       78-79
    freight-rate differentials, 67
    right-to-work laws, 47
    Taft-Hartley Act (1947), 47-48
    wage differentials, 49

Imperialist wars,
  Korean War, 159
  Spanish-American War, 38, 78
  Vietnam War, 159-60
  World War I, 11, 79, 59, 62
  World War II, 81-82, 59, 62
Industrial concentrations, 174
Industrial developments
  computers, 71-72, 95
  electronics, 71-72, 94-95, 98
  high technology, 63
Industrial periods, 60-63
Industrial shifts, 83
  aerospace, 94-95, 98
  apparel, 89-90, 173
  chemicals, 91-92
  defense, 94, 175
  electrical equipment, 94
  food processing, 91
  lumber and sawmill, 88-89, 173
  machinery, 90-91
  oil, 92-94
  party system periods and, 84
  power-loom textiles, 88
  railroads, 85-87
  slave-breeding, 84
  slave trade, 84
  smokestack industries, 70
  steel, 86
  textile spindles, 172
  textile wages, 46, 172
  transport equipment, 90-91
  water-powered textiles, 84-85
Inter-American wars, 18-21
  Brazil-Argentina-Uruguay War
    (1825-1828), 18
  Civil War in the U.S.
    (1861-1865), 19-21, 76, 146
  Ecuador-Peru War (1859), 18
  Mexican-American War
    (1846-1848), 18, 75, 146
  Pacific War (1879-1883), 18
  Paraguay War (1864-1870),
    19-21
  Uruguayan War (1839-1851), 18
Intermediate crises, 72, 169

1772, 73
1837-1843, 74
1873-1878, 76-77
1907, 80
1914-1915, 80
1920-1921, 63, 80
1937-1938, 63
1953-1954, 63
1973-1975, 63
International Workingmen's
  Association (IWA), 7-8
Irish question, 7-10, 118

Labor
  class interests, 100, 107
  exploitation, 97
  labor peace, 111
  movement, 138
  wage labor, 5, 150
Labor in crises, 100-107
  autoworkers, 106
  concessions, 106, 107, 110
  defensive reaction, 106
  garment workers, 106
  machinists, 106
  militancy, 111
  offensive action, 107
  rise and decline, 103
  rubberworkers, 106
  teamsters, 106
  unionized workers, 106
Labor legislation, 111
  National Labor Relations Act
    (1935), 110
  Taft-Hartley Act
    (1947), 110
Labor organizations
  AFL, 105-106, 152-53
  AFL-CIO, 47, 106-107, 166-67
  business unionism, 105
  CIO, 105-106, 109, 152-53
  city trade centrals (CTCs), 104
  city trade unions (CTUs), 103-104
  company unions, 105
  farm labor, 110
  Farm Labor Organizing
    Committee, 110

SUBJECT INDEX 197

industrial unions, 104-105
Industrial Workers of the
  World (IWW), 105, 109
Knights of Labor, 104-105
National Labor Union, 104
national trade unions
  (NTUs), 104
National Trades
  Federation, 104
Operation Dixie (1946), 47
revolutionary unions, 105
steelworkers, 109
Texas Farm Workers, 110
UAW, 106-107
United Farm Workers, 110
Labor repression
  American Nazi Party, 154
  conspiracy laws, 108
  conspiracy trials, 108
  cooptation, 113
  deportation, 109
  Haymarket Square Massacre
    (1886), 108
  injunctions, 110
  KKK, 154
  martial law, 108
  Memorial Day Massacre
    (1937), 109
  Palmer Raids (1920-21), 109
  Pinkerton detectives, 108
  right-to work laws, 47
  Taft-Hartley Act (1947),
    110, 128-29
Labor revolts, 107-12
  anthracite coal strike
    (1902), 109
  Bonus Army March (1932), 109
  canal workers strike
    (1830s), 108
  Chicago general strike
    (1886), 108
  coal strike (1946), 110
  conscious, 111
  Flint sit-down (1930s), 109
  Fries Uprising (1790s), 107
  general strikes, 108, 109
  Homestead steel strike
    (1892), 108
  J. P. Stevens strike, 154
  Molly Maguires, 108
  New England general strike
    (1860), 108
  Newport News Shipbuilding
    strike (1979), 154
  Pullman strike (1894), 109
  railroad strike (1877), 108
  rebellion, 108
  Shay's Rebellion (1780s), 107
  silver mines strike (1892), 108
  sit-down strikes, 109
  spontaneous, 111
  steel strike (1952), 110
  textile general strike
    (1930s), 109
  Tomkins Square rebellion
    (1874), 108
Labor vote, 110, 112
  electoral politics, 117
  state power, 115
  third party, 114
Land question
  class interests, 23
  conflict over, 23-30
  land claims, 22
  land speculation, 24
  Louisiana Purchase, 34
  Northwest Ordinance
    (1787), 24
  Ordinance of 1785, 24
  Public Domain, 22-24, 32, 39-40
  role of cotton gin, 24
  role of iron plows, 24

Manufacturers' Record, 46
Manufacturers
  Allis-Chalmers, 90-91
  Ampex, 94
  Arkwright Club, 46
  Chrysler, 62, 106, 110-11
  Ford, 106
  General Motors, 48, 79, 91,
    106, 109
  Goodyear, 48
  GTE Sylvania, 94

198 SUBJECT INDEX

Manufacturers, *continued*
  Litton Industries, 94
  Lockheed, 95
  Magnavox, 94
  National Cordage, 77
  relation to banks, 62
  Stackpole Carbon, 94
  Standard Oil, 78
  Texas Instruments, 95
  United States Steel, 81
  Western Electric, 95
Markets
  home, 19
  labor, 12
  national, 5
Materialist conception of history, 1-2
  evolutionary aspect, 2
  revolutionary aspect, 2
  structural aspect, 2
Multi-national state, 7, 50
  Canada, 10, 18
  United Kingdom, 6-11
  United States, 11-14

National development
  North, 35-37
  South, 25-30
  Western Hemisphere, 16-21
Nationalism
  chauvinism, 99, 152
  disruption of labor unity, 100
  ideological weapon, 9
  Northern, 37-41
  Southern, 31-35
National question
  history, 1-14
  Ireland, 7-10, 118
  racism and, 48
  separation of South, 117
National revolutions
  Brazilian Revolution (1810-1822), 17-18
  Canadian Rebellion (1837), 18
  Haitian Revolution (1790-1803), 17, 33-34

Latin American revolutions, 18
War of Independence, 73
Nations, 5, 16
  labor markets, 12
  rise of, 2-6
  town and country division of labor, 25
New York Tribune, 118
Northern imperialism, 68, 155
Northern labor movement
  chauvinism, 152
  history, 100-12
  new conditions, 163-68
Northern nation, 12, 117-18
  phases, 35
Northern national development, 35-37
  division of labor, 37
  home market, 37
  immigration, 35-36
  infrastructure, 36
Northern nationalism, 37-41
  tariffs, 37
Northern secessionism, 31-35
  Hartford Convention (1814), 35
  three movements, 34-5
Origins of the New South (Woodward), 15, 140
Parties: see *two-party system, third parties*
Party systems, 64, 65
  Civil War System, 66-68
  Democratizing System, 66
  Experimental System, 65
  Industrial System, 69
  New Deal System, 69
Planning for the South (Van Sickle), 89
Political crises, 100-107
Political-economic formations, 2
  bands, 3
  city-states, 4
  feudal domains, 4

nations, 5
socialism, 6
tribes, 4
Political-economic periods, 57
Political-economic
  realignments, 54-57
Political economy, 1
Political realignments, 56, 63-72
Political reserve
  Ireland, 9
  South, 100, 112, 140
Power Shift (Sale), 91, 96
Puerto Rico, 50

Quebec, 10, 13, 18

Racial discrimination, 48, 49
Railroads
  Erie, 78
  Northern Pacific, 77-78
  Philadelphia and
    Reading, 78
  Union Pacific, 78
Realignment cycle, 72
  crises and wars, 72-83
  economic programs, 72
  foreign policy, 82
  reforms, 78
  state power, 72
Realignments
  economy, 57-63
  politics, 63-72
Republican Party: see
  Two-party systems
Reserve
  South as economic, 41-58, 142
  South as political, 99-134
Revolution, 3, 97
  class confrontation, 110
  structural impediments, 2
Revolutionary conditions
  labor upsurge, 57, 102, 142
  political split in capital, 57, 101-103, 142
  Southern upsurge, 142
Revolutionary crisis, 102, 106

Secessionism
  Northern, 31-35
  Southern, 37-41
Slavery
  abolition, 28, 39
  abolitionist newspapers, 143
  Abolitionists, 42, 100
  basic economic law of, 31
  basis of capitalism, 54
  compensated
    emancipation, 124
  Dred Scott decision (1857), 39
  Emancipation Proclamation
    (1863), 59
  Fugitive Slave Act (1850), 39
  Kansas-Nebraska Act
    (1854), 34
  Missouri Compromise
    (1820), 34, 37
  Nicaraguan filibuster, 38
  Ostend Manifesto, 33, 38
  slave trade, 84-85, 119-20
  slave trade prohibition
    (1808), 85, 119
  Texas statehood (1845), 37-38
**Slavery and the Southern
  Economy** (Woodman), 19
Solid South, 113
  basis of, 137-39
  Dixiecrats, 133
Southern colonization, 12, 15, 41-50, 100
  freight-rate differentials, 67
  industry, 44
  infrastructure, 44
  national labor market, 45
  plantation economy, 44
  right-to-work laws, 47
  super-exploitation, 139
  Taft-Hartley Act, 47-48
  value of labor, 139
  wage differential, 47, 49
Southern labor movement
  control of, 142-54
  new conditions, 154-58
  Operation Dixie (1946), 47

200 SUBJECT INDEX

Southern nation, 12, 30, 118
Southern national
  development, 25-30
  core and border
    areas, 30, 98
  cotton production, 25
  culture, 135, 143
  division of labor, 25
  gospel, 143
  home market, 28, 43
  infrastructure, 28
  jazz, 143
  national literature, 15, 143
  phases, 25
  role of slavery, 25
Southern nation, 12, 30, 118
Southern nationalism, 31-35
  domestic policy, 32
  factors, 140-42
  filibusters, 32
  foreign policy, 33
Southern national movement,
    140, 142-54
  Alabama Sharecroppers
    Union, 152
  American Nazi Party, 154
  Civil Rights Movement,
    157-58, 165
  Colored Farmers National
    Alliance, 148
  condition of revolutionary
    crisis, 142
  dependency, 147
  KKK, 143, 154
  national inequality, 149
  national oppression, 148
  Negro people's movement,
    142-43, 165
  political factors, 140-42
  poor whites, 10, 143
  Populist movement, 150-51
  relief projects, 153
  sharecroppers, 146, 152
  Southern Farmers Alliance,
    148, 151
  Southern Tenant Farmers
    Union, 152-53
  territorial expansion, 145-46
  union drives, 154
  white workers, 138
  yeomen, 144
Southern Politics in State and
    Nation (Key), 128
Southern question, 118
  color, 135-68
  economic reserve, 51-98, 142
  international significance of,
    158-63
  labor suppression, 15, 142-54
  political reserve, 99-134
  U.S. economy and, 83-98
Southern Regions of the United
    States (Odum), 89
Southern secessionism, 37-41
  Confederate States of
    America, 16, 30, 39-40
  Secessionist Congress, 31
Southern strategy, 112-18, 131
  capital and, 131
  congressional seniority, 113-14
  control of labor, 132
  Judiciary Committee, 114
  legislative committees, 115
  role of Solid South, 113,
    127, 133
  two-party system, 131
State, 1
  multinational, 7, 50
  relation to capital, 107
  United Kingdom, 6-11
  United States, 11-14
Stocks
  Dow Jones Industrial
    Average, 80
  London Stock Exchange, 80
  New York Stock
    Exchange, 80

Theory
  practice and, 8
  realignments, 54-57
  Southern strategy, 112-18
Third parties, 107-12

SUBJECT INDEX 201

American Independent
  Party, 111
Citizens Party, 111
Farmer-Labor Party
  (1920), 111
Free Soil Party (1848), 111
Greenback Party (1876), 111
of labor, 111-12, 114-15, 176
Labor Party (1936), 111
labor vote, 112
Liberty Party (1839), 111
National Labor Reform Party
  (1872), 104, 111
Populist Party (1889), 111, 148
Progressive Party (1948), 111
state power, 115
States Rights Party, 111
Workingmen's Party
  (1828), 111
Two-party system, 119, 131, 134
capital and, 131
color question and, 155
party development, 119
Southern strategy and, 131
Two-party system before
  Reconstruction, 118-24
Abolitionists, 125
Civil War Party System, 66
coalition politics, 121
compensated
  emancipation, 124
Democratic-Republican
  Party, 121
Democratizing Party
  System, 66
disenfranchisement, 119
Experimental Party
  System, 65
Federalist Party, 120
Free Soil Party, 125
House of Representatives, 36
immigrant labor, 121
Jacksonian Democrats, 119
judiciary, 39
National Republicans, 120
national struggle, 131
protectionism, 120, 121

Republican Party, 122, 125
slavery question 122
Senate, 38
Southern Whigs, 124
Tammany Hall, 121
Virginia-New York
  Alliance, 121
Whig Party, 120, 124
Two-party system during
  Reconstruction
apportionment, 146
Civil War Party
  System, 67-68
martial law, 125
military governors, 43
military occupation of
  South, 123
Reconstruction governments,
  43, 123
Two-party system post-
  Reconstruction, 124-34
bribery and force, 132
capital accumulation, 132
Civil War Party System, 67
electoral commission, 126
ethnic vote, 130
Industrial Party System, 69
industrial policy, 126
internal improvements, 127
minority administrations, 126
Populist movement, 150-51
post-war industrialization, 53
revolutionary conditions, 124
Southern Whig
  Democrats, 125
Two-party system since
  New Deal
blacks, 133
bribery and force, 132
capital accumulation, 132
Dixiecrat-Republican
  alliance, 163
Dixiecrats, 133
ethnic vote, 130
fascism, 153
financiers, 133
foreign policy, 82

internal improvements, 127-28, 130
labor, 133
liberals, 133
New Deal Party System, 69
presidential tickets, 130
Solid South, 127, 133
Taft-Hartley Act (1947), 128-29

United States
economic realignments, 57-63
industrial concentrations, 174
multinational state, 11-14, 99-134
multinational economy, 51-98
national development, 15-50
political realignments, 63-72
two-party system, 118-34

Value added in manufacturing, 60-61

Wars, 72-83, 171
Barbary States, 74
Franco-Prussian War (1870), 11
Hawaii, 76
Indian wars, 75-76
inter-American wars, 18-21
for national independence, 17-18
realignment and, 72
Samoa, 76
War of 1812, 22, 35, 74
Western Hemisphere
colonization, 17
export economies, 19
home markets, 19
inter-American wars, 18-21
national development, 16-21
wars of independence, 17-18
WLAC (Nashville radio station), 135